Sparkle Island

stories of love, life, and Walloon Lake

Ellen Rosewall

Raven Tree Press

De Pere, Wisconsin

SPARKLE ISLAND
published by Raven Tree Press

©2000 by Ellen Rosewall

Edited by Jean Wentz and Daniele Burich
Copyedited by Amy Johnson
Book design by Laura Diedrick
Photo credits: Michael Rosewall, Ellen Rosewall, Lynne Hyatt Kishler,
Mary Lewis

Printed in the United States of America

For information:
Raven Tree Press, 100 S. Broadway, De Pere, WI 54115

Publisher's cataloging-in-Publication
(Provided by Quality Books, Inc.)

Rosewall, Ellen.
  Sparkle Island ; stories of life, love, &
Walloon Lake / by Ellen Rosewall — 1st ed.
  p. cm.
  ISBN 0-9701107-0-7

  1. Walloon Lake Region (Mich.) — Biography.
2. Rosewall family. 3. Rosewall, Ellen. I. Title.

F572.W24R67 2000   977.4'86
                 QB100-516

"The Test" © 1995 The Walloon Lake Villager. Reprinted by permission.

Printed on recycled paper.

FIRST EDITION

For Michael and Peter,
who give me a reason
to get up in the morning.

Acknowledgements

• • •

Truth be told, I've always found the acknowledgement pages of books to be a little self serving, like speeches on award shows. But when I finished writing this book, I found myself going through a grieving process. So since I want to keep writing just a little while longer, and there are indeed people to be thanked, I will proceed. I hope you will bear with me, because these are people who truly do deserve acknowledgement.

Most of the thanks in the world go to my wonderful assistant, Jean, who not only edits my work, remembers where I put the discs, knows how to operate all of the electronic equipment and occasionally even mops up after floods, but also puts up with the squawking of three birds who aren't always sure they like her. There is no job description in the world that can cover what Jean means to me and the work we do together.

Many thanks also go to Laura and Amy at Raven Tree Press, who not only agreed to publish the book but had the grace to be touched by it.

Thanks to Daniele, Dick and Diane, D.A., Anne and Beth, and other friends and family who read the stories and provided wonderful ideas which inspired more of them.

Thanks to my family for providing me with the material.

And special thanks to my Grandfather, Kenyon Campbell, who had the good sense and foresight to spend $1,000 in 1930 to create generations of memories that are just beginning. Grandfather, wherever you are, I hope you can read this.

Contents

· · ·

Introduction...

In September 24, 1900, Clyde Thurza Morford sold a parcel of land on the West Arm of Walloon Lake, near Petoskey Michigan, to Charles Wilhoit. Within a year, a modest cottage was built on the property. In 1907, Charley and Lulu Wilhoit sold the property to William and Walter Siddons, and in 1930, it was purchased by my grandfather, Kenyon Campbell, who named it Ja-Ma-Ca, in honor of his three daughters, Jane, Mary and Carolyn. Ever since then, it has remained in our family, passed from my grandfather to my mother upon his death. It is now jointly owned by my mother, my sisters Linda and Jan, and me.

Through births and deaths, marriages and separations, moves across the country and sometimes back again, career changes and life transitions, the cottage on Walloon Lake has been a magnificent constant, giving our family an anchor seldom found in today's mobile society. I may never be able to return to the house in Ohio I grew up in and see the marks on the wall that "immortalized" my growth spurts, but every summer I can lean over the dock and look for Petoskey rocks just as I've done every summer since I could walk. My family may never again live in the same town together during the winter months, but every summer we can congregate at the cottage, and it only takes a phone call to bring anyone who couldn't come into the fold.

This sense of place seems to be endemic to Walloon Lake. A few years back, the Walloon Lake Association held a contest to find the summer families who'd been on the lake the longest. Our family wasn't even in the top twenty-five. Along our little stretch of road, the same names have graced the mailboxes for generations (with some marriage-related variations), and to get there we drive along streets named for early residents like Morford and Depew. It's a phenomenon that has brought reporters from publications as diverse as *National Geographic* and *USA Today* here to try and determine what is so special, and how they can grab a piece of it.

Recently, we realized that an important anniversary was approaching: our cottage's one hundredth birthday and the new millennium would arrive simultaneously. An event of this magnitude is certainly something to be taken seriously, and we wanted to do something special to honor the occasion. We thought about putting up a plaque, or looking into National Historic Landmark designation, but that didn't appeal to us. After all, the cottage itself is only a part of our experience, and we didn't want to see it get all the glory.

To try and decide what to do, we sat down in front of the fire at the cottage and told stories about our life there. And in the course of the telling, it became clear that the stories themselves were the monument. They are the stories of our family, but they are also love stories, stories of growth, pain and change, and stories of shared laughter. They happen to have taken place at Ja-Ma-Ca, on Walloon Lake in northern Michigan, but they could have happened anywhere.

They are the cement which has held our family together, and will also, we are confident, hold our children and our children's children together. They are the stories of the past, and a gift to the future.

...Ellen

Sparkle
Island

Sparkle Island...

Last summer, a swan family moved into Mud Lake. We drove the boat down there several times to see the mom, dad and cygnet, who had the habit of coming right up to the boat looking for a handout. The shallow, reedy waters and the necessity of not disturbing the swans meant we had to travel very slowly. The whole world seemed to hold its breath back there where no jet-skiers dared to enter. The boat glided through the shallow waters like the swans did, and for a brief moment we were one.

"Look!" whispered Mom. "A sparkle island."

I don't recall ever hearing that term before, but I immediately recognized it. Sometimes on sunny days, when the water is very calm, a tiny little bit of wind will catch a piece of the surface in such a way that the sun will create a thousand dancing fairies. Amazingly, the area surrounding a sparkle island stays undisturbed, unaware of the light show right next to it. As you get close, the light changes and the sparkle island disappears, like the mirage of rain on a blacktop surface. But if you're lucky, another one will appear somewhere in front of you.

For most of the year, it is easy to miss sparkle islands. For most of the year we're like those jet-skiers, going fast and making lots of noise, not able to notice the special things that suddenly appear in front of us. Before we know it, we've passed over them and they're gone, and even if another one appears in the distance it too will soon be passed over without recognition of how special it is.

But for a few days, or weeks, during the summer, we drift slowly through the water. We can hear it closing over the oar that sinks below the surface. We spend hours on the front porch, feeling the breeze caress our skin and watching the birds, and not considering one moment wasted time.

Most of us have been going to Ja-Ma-Ca since we were babies. Some of us have joined later by marrying into the family. We've all been going long enough that all it takes is to step onto the front porch and we feel our muscles relaxing, our eyes opening, and our senses coming alive.

All of a sudden there are sparkle islands in every direction.

Mom had an appraisal done a few years ago to allow her to begin transferring ownership of Ja-Ma-Ca to us girls. When she showed me the report from the appraiser, I turned to the first page – there at the bottom of the page was an impressive figure along with the disclaimer, "as is." The use of the phrase which is normally attached to what we used to call a "handyman's special" intrigued me. So did the subsequent language that the home was being valued at 40% less than comparable properties because of the "superiority" of the other properties. What could this mean? I am a person who loves creature comforts and I had never thought that there was anything wrong with the cottage. Sure, it's old, but the bathrooms and kitchen are modern. Sure, we have to watch how many showers we take when the house is full, but nobody's ever had to go without, unless they wanted to (see Peter, ca. age 10). What could our shortcoming be?

Perhaps our bare floors or pressed-cardboard paneling were the culprits. I would hate to think so; they do have their benefits. One thing I've always loved about the cottage is that it seemed like it never needed to be cleaned. In all the years I had been there, a quick broom to the sandy floor or a shake of the rugs would suffice. The floor is a marvelous brown and rust linoleum that hides a multitude of sins. The ancient braided rugs undoubtedly carry remnants of my youthful trips up from the lake, but who cares? Unlike our homes in the city, which need constant dusting and vacuuming, I didn't remember any-one ever dusting the big fireplace or the wicker chairs.

A little dust, however, does not an "as is" make. I dug further, through the paragraphs that listed the four bedrooms, two baths, kitchen ("with improvements") and then I found it. In capital letters the appraiser had tersely listed our prime offense: "NO CLOSETS."

I had to think for a minute. Do we really have no closets? I guess we don't – the closet space consists of indentations of closet size and shape, with hanging rods, but with no doors enclosing them. Oh, and if you sleep in the back bedroom you have to make do with hanging your clothes on a makeshift rod on the back of the door, but that's okay, because the front bedroom has plenty of extra closet – oops, indentation – space if you need it. Enough extra space, in fact, to be able to house an assortment of rubber thong sandals that for many years included my Grandfather's, even though he died when I was in college.

Closets are an unnecessary frill, anyway. Closets are where you keep skeletons, and there's nothing about the cottage we need to shut the door on. Besides, during the day, you've got to have easy access to a variety of clothing. Once the second pot of morning cof-fee runs out, you've got to move quickly to get dressed or you might be left behind on the morning's walk or trip into town. Once the sun hits the dock in the afternoon, you wouldn't want to waste a minute of it searching for your bathing suit behind a closed closet door. And the evening air has been known to turn chilly in minutes – who has time to rummage on the closet floor for a sweater?

Appraisers aren't paid to consider the many benefits of not having closets. This may turn out to be a good thing, after all. Since we're never going to sell the cottage anyway, a house appraised at 40% below the neighbors just keeps the curious away. Fine with us. We have more important things to do.

Ernest Hemingway Sat Here...

I am sitting in a wicker chair. It is an unassuming chair, the kind found on the front porches of cottages like ours up and down the lake. It's an antique, probably over ninety years old, it sags a little, and a couple of loose ends of rattan threaten to break free and poke me in places I do not wish to be poked. But it is the perfect place to read a book and watch a sunset.

I am reading a book. It's an unassuming book, and it too is old, but younger than the chair. It is a book that sits in libraries, classrooms, and homes around the world, widely admired and celebrated. It is a book written by a man who once sat in this chair. Maybe.

It seems like Ja-Ma-Ca has always been ours, but before my Grandfather bought it in 1930, it was owned by two brothers from Marian, Indiana named William and Walter Siddons, AKA

"Windy Bill" and "Gloomy Gus." Although Walloon Lake was not nearly as populous as it is today, the Siddons had several neighbors, including a family a couple of miles down the road whose youngest child is the subject of this story.

Now it seems that in those days, it was somewhat of a coup to lay claim to the fastest boat on the lake, and for several years, the Siddons held that honor. Their beautiful launch, "Onward," had one of the first gasoline powered engines and was reputed to travel as fast as thirty miles per hour. This incredible feat earned them the duty of being fire marshals, traveling up and down the lake in times of emergency, notifying neighbors and collecting whatever resources, human or otherwise, were necessary for the occasion. When guests stepped into the boat, they sat on the wicker chairs that were the fashion for upscale launches of the day - the same wicker chairs that now sit on our front porch.

These things we know. What we do not know, but what we imagine, is that during one of the aforementioned emergencies, Windy Bill and Gloomy Gus hopped in the boat and went off searching for help. Stopping at the Hemingway cottage, they were greeted by a gentleman and his young son. "Can I come, too?" asked little Ernie. "Sure, hop in," said Windy Bill, and so the young lad clambered into the boat, eagerly claiming one of the wicker seats in the rear so he could watch lake and shore at the same time. The chair creaked a bit as Ernie leaned over to trail his fingers in the water, and while the adults were planning their rescue mission, stories of lakes and trees were spinning in Ernie's head. Once the emergency was over, the boat stopped back at the Siddons' and Ernie climbed up and down the broad steps of our front porch while the men relaxed, had a beer and enjoyed the sunset.

For most of my life, this tenuous connection to a famous writer has fueled my imagination in what I hoped was the same way

Ellen Rosewall

our cottage fueled Ernie's. I dreamed that when Ernie sat on our chairs or climbed up our steps it started a spark that would manifest itself in a story many years later. I hoped that something of that spark would also manifest itself in my stories; that the lake which had birthed one writer would be gracious enough to inspire another.

The truth is a little less romantic. There is no record of anyone in my family actually having any contact with the Hemingways after my grandfather purchased the cottage. For many years, the Hemingway cottage was occupied by Ernest's sister Sunny, who was, to use the media parlance, a "private person." We never met her, nor did we ever see her on any of our walks down the back road past her cottage, although she did surface every once in awhile to publish a memoir of the early days or a poetic tribute to the lake she loved as much as we do.

Sunny passed away a few years back, and her son, Ernest Hemingway Mainland, inherited the cottage. We heard a rumor shortly afterward that he was going to restore the cottage to the way it was when his uncle lived there, and we waited for the other shoe to drop, anticipating the diesel smell of the tour busses heading down our little road. But our fears, thankfully, turned out to be unfounded. Ernie Mainland opened the house to the public for a brief period when he assumed ownership, and again on the occasion of Hemingway's 100th birthday in 1999, but aside from that, Windemere has remained a private cottage.

We know that Ernest Hemingway is a public figure, but we have been grateful that Walloon and Windemere have remained for some reason largely untouched by the media mania that seems to have affected every aspect of the private lives of other famous people. Certainly one of the reasons we are grateful is that Walloon is our retreat, and we don't want it spoiled by traffic and gawkers. But hidden beneath that are secret fantasies of our family's theoretical brush

SPARKLE ISLAND

with greatness that have held onto for so many years and don't want to let go. We love to take our guests on a walk or drive and dramatically announce in hushed whispers that we are passing Ernest Hemingway's cottage as they search in vain for some kind of indication that we are correct (we're residents here, we just *know*). And the possibility definitely exists that if Ernie Mainland had thrown open the doors of Windemere, it would also have thrown open the doors of history to closer scrutiny and we would have found evidence that shattered all of our childhood myths of close ties between Ernie's house and ours.

Ernest Hemingway was a writer who embodied the axiom, "write what you know." After years of reading his terse, direct style, I admit that he would probably disapprove of my creating fanciful legends of something in our cottage inspiring one of his stories. I do have some consolation, however, in the fact that those chairs from the boat are very real. When I sit in one, it's hard not to imagine the thought of wicker marks on that famous backside all those years ago.

The Journey North...

My family and I feel so strongly about our time in Michigan that I believe we consider it the only "real" time of our lives. As we look back on our history, our time together at the cottage is the time when we formed the memories that mattered, experienced the feelings that counted, did the activities that deeply shaped us and our relationships with each other. It's hard to believe that all of this happened in only two weeks a year.

Even now, time is divided into two sections, "the cottage" and "everything else." During the "everything else" time, "the cottage" always somehow influences things. In the dead of winter, it's not unusual to run across some funny article in a magazine or a nicely shaped stone on the street and think, "I must remember to take that to the cottage with me." Buying clothes is always a project done with Walloon in mind. It's especially true with summer clothes, of course, but even an extra winter sweatshirt can be justified because it will do double duty on evening boat rides at the cottage. And of course, food purchasing and meal preparation for weeks in advance of leaving are done with the goal of making sure the refrigerator is empty by the time it's time to leave.

After almost fifty weeks of anticipation, the day that we leave for the cottage is so emotion-charged it's almost unbearable. When we were little, Mom and Dad would always have some kind of surprise for the trip, like a new game or toy, and often, like Christmas Eve, we would beg them to let us open it the evening before. I suspect they sometimes let us, just to ease the pressure a bit, but in my memory the day started with piling into the way-back of the station wagon and setting up what would be our play space for the next eight hours (for the horrified parents reading this, let the record show that we are all still alive), squealing with delight at our surprises. The games and toys would last throughout much of Ohio, even part of southern Michigan, but as we got north of Detroit and the terrain started to change, the familiar feelings would come rushing back and we paid more attention to the trees and the occasional glimpse of water than we did our Barbie™ dolls and Travel Bingo.

Somewhere around Flint we started to see the signs advertising Sea Shell City. We imagined it to be the Eighth Wonder Of The World, so grandiose were the claims made on the billboards. One year we counted them – one-hundred-twenty-seven in all, probably the sole advertising investment of the enterprise, geared to gradually build the frenzy of children traveling north with their parents until their parents were forced to stop just to shut the kids up. I think my Dad must have distracted us just as we passed Sea Shell City, because it wasn't until I was much older, at least in junior high, that I realized that the place was not all it claimed to be. By that time I didn't care to stop, anyway. It wouldn't have been cool.

Gradually, as we got further north, we saw fewer signs for fast food and more pine trees. The air began to get cleaner, or at least we imagined it did, and even if we had left 90 degree temperatures in the city we knew we would have a fire in the fireplace to ward off the chill lake air by that evening. We started to see familiar sights: The Sugar Bowl restaurant in Gaylord, Boyne Mountain Ski Area. We began the annual argument of whether or not we should stop at the Village of Walloon Lake to lay in some supplies before heading to the grocery store the next day. Despite our desire to be there, we usually stopped. But just for a minute. And an ice cream cone.

And then, there we were. It looked the same as last year, or the year before. We rushed out of the house, down the steps, and around to the front to say hello to the lake. We were home.

Nowadays, I come to the cottage via the northern route, up and over Lake Michigan through the Upper Peninsula and down across the Mackinac Bridge. Since I live in Green Bay, which is right at the juncture between the rolling southern farm country and the north woods, we only have to travel for a few minutes before my head begins to clear and I feel like I'm almost there. I have the luxury of traveling for over five hours through some of the most gorgeous country on earth; the clean sand and clear blue waters of Lake Michigan on my right, seemingly endless stretches of white pine and quaking aspen on my left. We have new familiar landmarks, the first view of the Mackinac Bridge as we make the turn into St. Ignace arguably the best of them. But I still plan the trip for weeks just as I've done for more than forty years. I still buy a new sweatshirt, and plan the refrigerator cleanout with great gusto.

And I still take a peek into my goody bag the night before we leave, hoping that there's a new crossword puzzle book I can get started on just a little early.

ISLAND SPARKLE

DEAR LAKE

...

Dear Lake,

Some kids write in their diaries or notes to their friends but I feel like if I write to you, it's like someone is really listening and it's not like a person who could tell someone else or stuff. Sometimes I feel like you're like a person anyway. Every summer (you probably know) the first thing we do when we get to the cottage, we have to say hello to you. Even before we get inside and see if Grandma left us any gumdrops in the corner cupboard.

Sometimes when I'm in my bed at home and I have bad dreams, my mommy comes in and touches my hair and tells me to think about the lake. So I lie there and look at the ceiling and I think about you and I can almost see you, smooth like glass, like when I come downstairs in the morning. Or I can feel what it feels like to float on my back with my eyes closed and my ears are under water, and it feels like there's nobody but me in the whole world. Or I can imagine that I'm really in my bed at the cottage, because when I'm there I can always go right to sleep listening to the waves coming up over the rocks. Somebody told me that that sound was called "lapping." That sounds good to me because it's like rocking in mommy's lap.

Here's something you probably don't know. We always play a game when we're first getting to the cottage. When we turn down the road by the Christmas trees, we pretend like we're going to give a prize to the first person to see you. When we get to the top of the hill, and we can see the first sign of blue, we all shout out together. So nobody wins the contest but it's fun anyway.

I guess this is really silly but who cares.

Love,

me

I'm Hamesucken and I Can't Get Up...

I don't know why it is so much fun to play games at the cottage. In two weeks, there is more serious game playing than all the rest of the year combined, and there is practically no time of day when someone isn't playing something. It starts shortly after breakfast when the second pot of coffee is brewed and the Yahtzee™ game comes out. It continues through the day when crossword puzzle books can be found on various tables inside and on the porch. And it usually continues far into the night, when we join in playing games together in the living room or split up into smaller groups for Boggle™ (usually Linda and Michael squaring off in the annual championship OF THE WORLD) or cards.

For people who laugh as much as we do when we're playing games, we're pretty serious about it. A lesser family would have crumbled over the nasty "is *loden* a word" incident. A few years back, we bought a dictionary at the used book store that weighs at least twelve pounds (I can't imagine why someone got rid of it). It was immediately christened the "Big Dic," and has become the official, final word on all disputes. If a word is not in the Big Dic, it does not exist. Unfortunately, so many words DO exist in the Big Dic that one can simply put down combinations of letters like "ert" and "nug," and chances are pretty good that you'll get the points. We're thinking of instituting a rule that if you write a word (especially Michael), you actually have to know what it means. The only reason we haven't is because Michael says that rule would be fine with him. That's because he's discovered that nine times out of ten, your obscure word will turn out to be defined as a "food fish."

Of course, we only use the rules when they serve our purpose. Most of our evening games, for instance, are played without benefit of scorekeeping or even the game board – we just pass around the trivia card box. Sometimes we get really fancy and insist that whoever answers a question correctly gets to ask the next one. But since that involves getting out of your chair to give the box to the next person, it is not a common practice.

The evening games, played by everyone available to the accompaniment of crackling logs in the fireplace or a thunderstorm over the lake, are just about the most fun it is possible to have. I have often thought that if some enterprising social scientist wanted an example of the embodiment of the phrase "quality family time," they should join us in a game of Balderdash™. Not many evening games go by without some silly answer or turn of events that has us shaking with laughter (in Linda's case) or tears running down our faces.

Our eccentricities are not limited to word games, though. It is a fact that Grandpa Charlie has saved the score sheets from every Yahtzee game he has ever played. They are carefully dated, and you

Ellen Rosewall

can tell the ones he won because there is a big red magic marker star at the bottom by his score. Mom's wins merit a small red star, and we kids are lucky if we get acknowledged. We have fought back against Charlie's Yahtzee chauvinism by bringing a hand-held electronic Yahtzee game to the cottage. It's addictive, but not as much fun.

Oh, the title of this essay? Kind of hard to explain, but it involves the aforementioned quality time, Balderdash, and shaking with laughter.

Petoskey Stones...

There was a coral that inhabited the earth millions of years ago...more accurately, it didn't inhabit the whole earth, it just inhabited a small area around what is now known as Petoskey, Michigan. It makes a very unusual and attractive fossil, and is found in abundance along the shores of Lake Michigan and a few inland lakes in the vicinity, including Walloon. It doesn't seem to be found anywhere else on earth, and although it is not by any stretch of the imagination a precious stone, it has brought quite a bit of gold to area merchants.

You can find just about anything made with Petoskey stones in Petoskey, ranging from the attractive (single stones set in necklaces or rings) to the bizarre (in the shape of the state of Michigan adorning a bolo tie). I personally have never seen anyone purchase the bolo ties or the ones in unusual shapes, and I suspect some of the same stones have been sitting in Grandpa Shorter's General Store since I first saw them in 1955 or so. They just dust them every once in awhile in the hope that they look new enough to entice some newcomer: "Look, Herman, there's this strange coral that is unique to this area, I sure would love some in the shape of a turtle." I can't imagine that happening very often, but that's probably why I haven't made my fortune in the souvenir business.

We have had a wonderful collection of Petoskey stones over the years. You'd think we would have bagsful by now, but like people living next to a diamond mine, we can afford to be picky. We don't wade in the shallow water on calm days any more due to the swimmer's itch, but we still hang over the dock, keep a sharp eye on the side of the road during our daily walks (Linda is especially good at this), or go to the beach near Nine Mile Point and gather several each year. Some are thrown back into the lake or back to the side of the road immediately, weeded out due to an inferior fossilization or blemish (these are the ones we probably find again the following year). The best are sorted out at the end of the summer and only our favorites kept. The creme de la creme, the very, very best, are given the honor of being covered with clear nail polish and becoming part of the permanent collection.

As valuable as they seem to be in the Petoskey area, they are not a big hit when we give them to friends at home. Perhaps there is something in the way the sun glints off of your eyes in Petoskey, but they just don't seem as cool when you take them away. Kind of like a movie that you watch because it's set in a place that you've visited, but after it's over you realize that, although it was fun to spot familiar scenes, you wouldn't rent it on video.

Those stones just don't seem at home anywhere else. They knew a good thing when they saw it, even millions of years ago.

Ellen Rosewall

The Petanque Court...

When we were kids, our little stretch of Lake Grove Road was filled solidly with summer cottages, but beyond Depew Road, there were long stretches of unclaimed lakefront. Gradually the 'for sale' signs went up; gradually they went down again and the earth movers dug into the land, sometimes mercifully down the bank toward the lake. For the newer homes were built by those who didn't care to be close to the road. We could tell that they were different, though, because close to the road we began to see garages. Few of the summer homes had garages; they were only needed in harsh weather. The building of the year-round homes had begun.

These weren't just year-round homes, either. They were year-round homes built by people who could afford to purchase a couple of acres of increasingly desirable lakefront property, more valuable than other lakes because of its cleanliness and proximity to a nice-sized town. More valuable even than Lake Michigan, because you could swim and operate small boats in it.

It was inevitable that shortly after the garages came, they became fruitful and multiplied. Two stall garages led to three and four and even six stall garages, built to store all of the owners' multiple land and sea vehicles (too bad we didn't know which ones the jet-skis were stored in, or they might not have needed so many garages). When the new properties had pretty much reached the limit on number of garages, they started outdoing their neighbors by building tennis courts.

It is difficult, even in the country, to find enough space for multiple garages and tennis courts without cutting down so many trees that the point was more or less lost. So, the next logical step involved condominium communities which provided all of the amenities that people of means have come to expect.

As I write, there is in the works on nearby Little Traverse Bay a miraculous undertaking. It is called Bay Harbor, and it is an entire community built from scratch with every possible luxury and convenience: a complete 18-hole golf course, wildlife sanctuary, private yacht slips, tennis courts, equestrian club... probably even closets. Property is so expensive it is rumored that Madonna and Arnold Schwarzenegger have purchased homes there. We went there once to drive around but were only allowed in as far as the sales office.

We keep a low profile at Ja-Ma-Ca. We don't want the word to get out, for what we have is even more exclusive than the sparkling facilities at Bay Harbor.

We have, to our knowledge, the area's only petanque court.

For most of the time, the court is cleverly disguised as a gravel driveway. We don't want to attract attention. But, sometimes we move the cars over to the other side of the road, and get out the wooden box that cradles our treasured boules, couchonnets and string. Petanque, the French equivalent of bocce ball, is one of those perfect games that combine skill and luck with an old-world style that seems to come as easily to newcomers as it does to the earthy, French-speaking veterans we've watched on the real petanque courts in Sonoma, California and Washington, D.C.

The walkers on the road admire the way the heavy metal boules, released from the underside of the hand, soar through the air and land with a graceful "thunk," hopefully nearer to the couchonnet than the one previously thrown (the distinctive sound of the ball hitting the turf has led Charlie to surmise that the English translation of "petanque" must be "ker-plunk."). I'm sure they don't realize that they are watching the most skilled petanque players on Walloon Lake. Probably, and I'm going way out on a limb here, in the entire Little Traverse Bay area.

We might let Arnold play there. For a small fee.

Food Fads...

They say that on vacation, all diet bets are off. No family has ever embraced that maxim with as much enthusiasm as we have. It started out years ago with the need to make an annual pilgrimage to our favorite of the many local fudge shops. At some point, however, we began to scorn fudge, probably when locals started calling the tourists "fudgies." But the sugar was in the system, as they say (or should), and we soon found other sinful habits in which to indulge.

We still go to Kilwin's fudge shop, but these days we go for the ice cream – so rich you can practically see the butterfat, crammed deeply into waffle cones too big for young children to handle. We gaze scornfully toward the tourists at the fudge counter as we dig into flavors like "Mackinac Island Fudge," "Traverse City Cherry" and "Bear Paw." Somewhere along the line we came to the unspoken conclusion that getting right back into the car and going home would be too obvious. So, we walk around the Gaslight District in Petoskey's downtown, window shopping or planning tomorrow's shopping trip. We have recently heard that tourists are now called not only fudgies but "cone-suckers," but we like our ice cream so much we don't even care.

Cherries are the area's most notable crop, but although we indulge, we are not prone to stopping frequently at the cherry stands that appear every mile or so along Highway 31. For many, the just-picked cherries are an irresistible delight. We'd rather have them in pie. Jespersen's Cherry-Berry pie. Preferably with Kilwin's ice cream on top. We love Cherry-Berry pie so much that Mom and Charlie once drove from Columbus, Ohio to Green Bay, Wisconsin by way of Petoskey so we could have one for Thanksgiving dessert. They even had to stay at a motel, because the cottage was closed for the winter, but boy, was that pie good.

Now, I know what you're thinking, but we're outside all day, doing healthy, active things, so these indulgences don't count...much. Besides, we give equal time and gusto to foods that even Richard Simmons would approve. Long before baby carrots were found in every grocery store, we went to the vegetable stand on the bluff atop Harbor Springs to get the "darling" veggies – carrots, potatoes and baby peas that were picked in their infancy and height of sweetness. This stand also adopted a practice that we thought was an excellent marketing tool – they set up mini sprinklers in the midst of the pro-duce, which would periodically spray a fine mist over the carrots, beets and sweet corn. I still remember their magnificent displays which made the vegetables seem as rich as ice cream, and even though many grocery stores today do the same thing, in my mind there is no corn more golden, no peas greener than those at Bluff Gardens.

The lazy days of summer afford us lots of time to explore farmer's markets and roadside vegetable stands, and we've tried 'em all. We know where to watch for the "fresh sweet corn" signs and who has the best zucchini. There's a family-run operation near our house that for a couple of years operated on the honor system – their wares were displayed on a picnic table, and customers weighed their own and left their money in a cup. Recently, they had staff outside again, a move I would like to interpret as meaning that they were successful enough that they could afford to hire someone.

Also appearing on the "healthy" side of the menu (although not as far to that side as fresh vegetables) is the local specialty, planked whitefish. Fresh whitefish from Lake Michigan is surrounded by Duchess potatoes (mashed potatoes squeezed in wavy blobs from a pastry bag), topped with lemon slices and a couple of tomato wedges, and broiled until the edges of the fish and potatoes turn brown and crispy, and the lemon flavor soaks into the fish. Wow. We seldom wait more than twenty-four hours after arrival to head to Juilleret's in Harbor Springs for this unequaled delicacy.

We have emerging food fads, like Steve's homemade cinnamon rolls, and failed food fads, like whitefish paté. I'm sure we'll go through many more. But nothing will ever taste as good as Mackinac Island Fudge ice cream in the twilight under a gaslight in downtown Petoskey, unless it is ice cream preceded by a plankful of whitefish.

The Fireside Club...

In September 1, 1923, the Fireside Club was formed. I'm sure when my grandfather joined, he was looking for a good time, a little drinking and other mild shenanigans away from the womenfolk. I can just imagine how they would laugh to hear that one of their descendants was writing about them over seventy-five years later. But then, as I understand it, they laughed at just about anything.

The Fireside Club started out as a group of fraternity buddies recently graduated from Ohio State University who decided to vacation together. Their intentions were hardly serious – after all, the members included men whose nicknames were Pike, Pewee, Pittenheimer and Nippy – but they were also future lawyers and businessmen and I don't suppose they could help trying to bring a little order to the proceedings.

By 1929, they had incorporated, sent out regular newsletters to members and had added a Midwinter Festival back in Ohio. The summer headquarters were at Goosepimple Lodge, Pike and Pewee Brown's cottage on Walloon Lake (named not for the obvious, but for a small tin lamp hung from the ceiling with poked-nail holes, which caused small goosepimple-like dots of light to be strewn across the room).

As you can imagine, their exploits were legendary, at least among themselves. Some were no doubt considered too much for delicate feminine ears, but a few have come down to us, like the time Tracy "Pittenheimer" Pittenger (my mother's uncle) was serenading one of the local girls in the boat with his piccolo and dropped it (the piccolo, that is) in the lake. Why he was playing a piccolo, just what he was doing to make it fall into the lake, and whether or not the young lady stuck around after that is unrecorded.

By 1930, seven years of vacationing at Walloon Lake had woven its spell on my grandfather. He was married with a family by that time, and he and my grandmother decided to vacation at Crystal Lake near Frankfurt and visit Pike Brown as part of the vacation. When they arrived at Goosepimple Lodge, Pike informed them that a cottage down the street was about to come out of probate and be put up for sale. Grandfather and Grandmother went down, walked around the boarded-up cottage, and bought the property without ever seeing the inside. That action was the beginning of the end of the Fireside Club (hard to work up to the revelry level of previous years with a wife and three young children about), but it started a new adventure we've been living ever since.

My mother was four years old when her family packed up their vacation gear at Crystal Lake and moved into their new cottage. Kenyon "Nippy" Campbell, my grandfather, paid a grand total of $1,000 for his lakefront treasure – land, cottage and furnishings.

Much of the original furniture is still in the cottage. And my mother still has the incorporation papers for the Fireside Club, just in case. Not a bad investment, all things considered.

DEAR LAKE

●●●

Dear Lake,

Just one more week of school left. We had our choir concert today and I got to sing a solo in front of everybody. No other girls had solos but they let Nicholas play his clarinet. Once Mrs. Kolodzik let me play a song from my piano lesson but just for the class.

I like playing the piano a lot, but after today I think I might like singing better. Every time I play the piano for somebody my hands shake and it makes me miss notes. Today when I sang, my knees shook a little bit, but they don't show, and my voice wasn't nervous most of the time. And I got to look at the audience, and see if they smiled or not, and that made it easier.

I've been thinking, wouldn't it be cool if we made a show at the cottage? I think the boathouse would be really great for a stage. We could have everyone sit facing the lake. Janice is too little to be in it, but I think Linda would be okay. We could sing songs from school and Girl Scouts and we could ask everybody to come, Aunt Do and Uncle Allen and the Kreinbihls and everybody. Maybe Anne could be in it.

Would you like that?

Love,

me

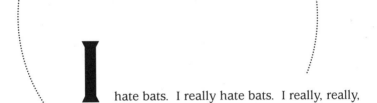

Bats...

I hate bats. I really hate bats. I really, really, really hate bats.

I know, don't tell me. Bats are good creatures. With the exception of vampire bats, which don't even exist in the United States, they only rarely bite humans. They can eat up to half their weight in insects in one night, and in some parts of the United States huge shelters are built so that bats will move in and save the crops. I also understand that bat guano is valuable enough that it is mined and sold for fertilizer, but I don't even want to get into that.

The bats I see swooping through the trees at night at the cottage are probably eating the mosquitoes that would have bitten me the next day. They have digested those mosquitoes and the result is undoubtedly responsible for the rich plant life we enjoy every day.

Fine. Just don't get me near one.

This past summer, I noticed some dirt on the floor of the front porch underneath the rolled up blind. Closer inspection revealed it to be the aforementioned bat guano. Of course, Peter was mightily intrigued by this, and rolled down the blind to reveal a bat, which promptly flew away, causing me to move my crossword puzzle book to the other side of the porch for the duration of our stay. Jan reminded me that this had happened before, several years ago, which does not give me confidence to resume sitting over there. The view is better from the north side of the porch, anyway. You can see the whole dock and even get a glimpse of any ducks who happen to be swimming by. And, if I want to see the goldfinches at the birdfeeder, I can always go inside and use the binoculars.

Bats also reside under the eaves at Kilwin's, which we know, of course, because we spend so much time there. I don't know why no one has happened to think about the fact that we are eating ice cream while staring up at the Kilwin's bats. "Look, there are five tonight," we say, and point them out to any young children who happen to be passing by. Unlike others, however, I keep a close eye on my ice cream while doing this, especially if it's cookies and cream.

While doing the extensive research that is the hallmark of these essays, I did discover one fact about bats that I find intriguing. Between May and July, females of some bat species mate, then kick out the males and go do some bonding in a cave. Hundreds of bat-moms then happily give birth, each one producing a single pink, naked, blind baby. This all would be good enough, but then the new mothers hang the babies up by their feet and fly away, leaving the babies to find their own way in the three or so months it takes them to mature.

This gives me a whole new perspective. But, until someone figures out how to determine the gender of bats from 40 feet away, I'm still not going to sit on the south side of the porch.

Lost In The Lake...

If some enterprising local nonprofit organization ever wants to schedule an interesting fundraiser, they might think of dredging the lake for treasure. If my family history is any indication, there's quite a lot of stuff to be discovered out there.

It takes those of us who live on land most of the year a little while to get used to the fact that water has a completely different set of rules. By the time we've gotten our summer sea legs, we've experienced a number of mishaps. I'm sure any serious study would prove that most bee stings and sunburns occur during the first few days of vacation. That's also the time when we tend to lose things in the lake.

For me, it started when I was about four and had not yet heard that the water was a cruel mistress. My toy *du jour* was an empty coffee can, and I was dragging it in the water as we rode in the boat. Of course, the strength of the water was too much as the boat got faster in the deep water, and down went my coffee can, never to be seen again. In death, the coffee can became my most treasured possession, and I wept bitterly as my grandmother put her arms around me and, showing no sympathy, gently told me "that's what happens when we don't keep our hands in the boat."

We've already heard about the Fireside Club and the lost piccolo, but believe it or not, my father dropped an entire boat motor in the lake. I don't remember details like why he was holding a boat motor in his arms in the middle of the lake, but I do remember looking over the side and hearing the "swoosh-ploop!" as the water closed over it. It must have been a spare one, though, because I don't remember having to paddle back. I think I would have remembered that, because I know my assistance with the oars would have been required, no matter what my age.

My husband was initiated into cottage life on our honeymoon, and he has had an amazingly good attitude about it over the years, considering that one of the first things he did at Walloon was to lose his wedding ring during an afternoon swim. Yes, the cold water does cause shrinkage of some body parts. I guess I can give thanks that on our honeymoon, the only affected body part was his finger. We searched for days with no luck, so we can only hope that the ring is covered by layers of sand and did not choke some poor fish.

Unfortunately, we occasionally see other items at the bottom of the lake or washed up on the shore, like beer cans and plastic bags. When those sets of plastic rings that hold together soda and beer six-packs first came out, we saw a lot of those on the beach, and we showed our ecological concern by picking them up and cutting them apart so they wouldn't wind up around the neck of a duck. We know that the lake hides a great deal of human debris: some dropped acci-

Ellen Rosewall

dentally and mourned by someone, more discarded casually by those who can't seem to learn the difference between a lake and a wastebasket.

Perhaps the lake will accept our sacrifice of treasured toys and wedding rings and be understanding of those who show less respect.

Modern Conveniences...

There is a strange dichotomy in cottage mystique. When you pick up regional magazines, they always show pictures of "cottages" containing at least $50,000 worth of furniture, artwork, and designer expertise in the living room alone. Apparently, selling magazines is predicated on the myth that getting away from it all is linked with being wealthy enough to enjoy the good life while you're gone. On the other hand, there are those who have grown up with memories of primitive summer adventures and swear that it's not a true cottage unless you drink out of jelly jars and sit in wicker furniture with broken ends of the rattan stabbing you in uncomfortable places.

Although our cottage admittedly leans much farther toward the jelly jar end of the spectrum, none of us is particularly interested in putting up with unnecessary deprivations just for form's sake. We still have linoleum floors, a screen door that bangs shut, and the afore-mentioned wicker chairs. We even have an assortment of jelly jars, collected by my grandmother when they were just the right size for breakfast juice. But we also have a dishwasher and microwave oven.

Jan fought the microwave oven, though. Bigtime. Modernizing the kitchen is one thing, but Jan's argument was that if we can live with strange bugs in the bathroom and carting our clothes to the laundromat in Petoskey, we can certainly wait until our dinners are cooked the old fashioned way.

Bull, said Mom. Retirement is for relaxing and doing what's important, and I'm not going to spend my summers in the kitchen when there are birds to be watched. She did have a point, having grown up in an era when she was required to spend most of her time in the kitchen no matter if she was at the cottage or at home. Our romantic memories of singing campfire songs while experimenting on a new cookie recipe probably lived in Mom's mind as one more messy kitchen she had to clean up after we went down for a swim.

For many years, the cottage had no indoor plumbing, and the privy was located across the street in the woods. For someone whose own personal "indoor plumbing" works 24 hours a day, I find this impossible to imagine, and I profoundly thank my grandmother who I assume was the one who drew the line at this atrocity. During my childhood, even the trip downstairs in the middle of the night was frightening, because you never knew if a Daddy Long Legs had man-aged to sneak in earlier in the day. Thank goodness, we now have an upstairs bathroom too. It's even been remodeled (the year after the microwave) and now has a shower that doesn't leak and tile that matches the floor.

One of the best examples of the primitive/modern schizo-phrenia we enjoy is the presence of Charlie's fax machine, which sits on the same table with the address book that still contains telephone numbers with letter-designated exchanges and the guest book whose first entry was made in 1948. Nowadays, we even use the copy function of the fax to share recipes, instead of spending our afternoons copying by hand onto index cards like we used to.

Heating is the only aspect of cottage life that still has a primitive aspect as well as a modern alternative. When we think of chilly nights, we most normally yearn for the big stone fireplace, but as romantic as it is the fireplace scores poorly on the practical meter. Like most fireplaces, much of the heat is felt within a few feet, and people sitting on the other side of the room are still shivering under afghans. So, in the 50s, a big oil furnace was installed. It stood in the living room opposite the fireplace, and you started it by opening the metal door, stuffing in newspapers and lighting them. It was smelly and smoky, took up most of the living room, and probably more dangerous that we were willing to admit, so we were thrilled in 1979 when Mom finally got rid of it and installed an LP gas heater, with the tanks outside and unobtrusive floor vents. The LP gas also has the advantage of starting by itself, just by raising the thermostat, and heating the downstairs in a matter of minutes. It is not vented upstairs, however, so we still have the primal pleasure of snuggling under layers of blankets to ward off the often chilly night air.

Modern conveniences or primitive living – where do you draw the line? It's quite simple, really. I believe that the people who long for primitive living are really looking for something else. It's not the jelly jars, it's getting away from the complications of modern society. It's something that we've found just by being together and looking at sunsets. It's something real enough to survive even a microwave oven.

SPARKLE ISLAND

Sunset Pictures...

Many of the original cottages on Walloon Lake face west. This is because an unknown quirk of nature has created the ideal conditions for nature's most incredible sunsets. From our cottage, we can sit on the boathouse or the dock and watch the sun going down over a ridge right across the lake. When the clouds are right, the orange streaks spread across the sky and reflect on the water all the way to our dock.

Since long before there was color film, we have been trying to capture this phenomenon with our cameras. I remember taking my first sunset pictures with a camera that had its viewfinder on the top. We've taken them with everything from instant cameras to manual focus 35mm ones with fancy lenses. We even took a panoramic camera up one year and got a beautiful shot of the entire opposite shore.

The planning starts at about 4:00 in the afternoon, when the sun has started its downward journey across the lake and we are contemplating packing up our sunscreen and heading back up to the house. Being experienced sunset photographers, we know by then if the cloud formations in the sky have potential. "Gonna be a good sunset," someone will say, and the watch is officially on. From then until dusk, everyone keeps glancing back at the sky every few minutes, charting the movement of the clouds in relation to the setting sun. When the time comes, no words need be exchanged. We all just grab our cameras and head for the boathouse or the dock and aim toward the promise: this time, we'll get the same thing on film that we see in person.

One year, Jan and Linda and I walked down to Hoffman's Point, even though it is private property and we aren't supposed to. From that vantage point, we had an unobstructed view of the entirety of the sunset, whereas at the cottage we sometimes get trees in the way. The pictures were okay, but they weren't from our dock, and we never went back. Our photo albums back home are by now crammed with various pictures of orange skies, and we can't even tell what year they were taken. Nevertheless, we still keep clicking away.

I don't think anyone has noticed, but I haven't taken any sunset pictures for the past few years. You see, I realized at one point that by hurrying down to the dock and trying to get just the right angle with my camera I was actually missing the sunset. I also realized that looking at those pictures at home never gave me the same feeling. A good sunset is like a Brahms symphony. It starts slowly, but you can feel the anticipation building. It takes a long time, and when the peak comes, you sometimes don't even realize it, because the waning is just as beautiful. The payoff is worth every minute you spent huddled in your jacket trying to ignore the chill of the night air.

Ellen Rosewall

Humans create beautiful works of art and put them in museums, galleries and homes where we can enjoy them again and again. This is good, but Nature has a different modus operandi. Every day, she creates a new work of art. If you miss one today, that's okay. There will be another one tomorrow. The catch is, you have to be looking.

Michael and I purchased a new camera last Christmas, one with manual focus and changeable lenses. When we opened it, the first thing that came to my mind was the definitive sunset picture. Maybe I'll have to take just one more.

Good Reasons to Take a Walk

1. To look for Petoskey stones
2. To identify as many species of wildflower as possible
   (no picking allowed, of course)
3. To dream dreams and to share them with someone you love
4. To see if there's a pickup whiffle-ball game in the meadow
   across from Stream's End
5. To go to the top of the hill and look out over the lake
6. To see if anyone else is out walking
7. To see who's arrived, who's gone home, and who's still here
8. To go all the way to the Inkwell House
9. To show a visitor the Hemingway cottage
10. To find out where that woodpecker noise is coming from
11. To find out where that wood burning smell is coming from
12. To see how far you can go before it starts raining
13. It's not warm enough to swim
14. To see if anything has changed since last year
15. To scope out the new neighbors
16. To see if the cattails in the marsh have burst open yet
17. To take some pictures
18. Because everyone is going

Bad Reasons To Take A Walk

1. To get some exercise

DEAR LAKE...

Dear Lake,

Only one more week until we get to see you, and only six more weeks until I'm officially in high school!

I've already planned for the trip. I bought a new *Seventeen* magazine, and I only cheated and read a little of it. I can't wait to plan my fall clothes. I'm going to need a new v-neck sweater, and Mom's going to sew me a new skirt in Campbell plaid to go with it. It will look so cool! Everyone's been talking about that new liquid eyeliner, and I think I'll buy some when I get there and try it out. That way if it looks bad nobody will see me.

I think I'll tell Lez my address and Terri, but not Carol. Maybe I'll get a letter from Darin! Do you think so? That would be so cool. It's fun to get mail at the cottage, even though we're only there two weeks. It seems like forever till I see my friends again.

We have to read a book for summer reading, so I've picked *Rebecca*, by Daphne du Maurier. Lez read it and said it was cool. This year, I am definitely going to plan my tanning so that I get tan all around my legs. You have to turn your legs to the sides, otherwise you end up with a white stripe up each side. I learned *that* the hard way last summer and it was so gross. Anyway, I can take my book down to the dock, it won't be that bad.

I wonder if we can get WLS on the radio again this summer? It is so cool that you can get a Chicago station so far away. Petoskey has *no* radio stations.

Love,

me

Entrepreneurs...

Sometime in the early 50s, my grandfather on my father's side visited the cottage and wrote in the guest book that "Walloon air acts like a sleeping pill." I've read that sentence probably a hundred times over the years as I leafed through the guest book. But it never dawned on me to bottle that air and sell it.

When I worked at Glacier National Park one summer in college, I sat by a waterfall the day before I left for home, turned my little portable tape recorder on and let it go until the tape ran out. I listened to that tape over and over, when I missed the outdoors in the middle of winter, when I needed help concentrating on my studies, or just when I felt blue. I even played that tape in Peter's crib when he was a baby, the only thing that would soothe him to sleep, until it finally wore out and broke after years of constant use.

S P A R K L E   I S L A N D

But it never occurred to me that this might be a marketable idea.

Recently, Michael and I went window shopping at an urban galleria in downtown Chicago, where I saw an interesting toy in one of those upscale gadget shops. It looked like a small stereo speaker and it had several buttons on the front, labeled "rainfall," "forest," "ocean," and "birds." I put on the headphones and pressed "rainfall." Almost immediately the delicate sound of raindrops hitting the ground filled my ears. I closed my eyes and could almost see rain dripping off leaves, splashing on the roof and running in rivulets down a crack in the soil. I pressed "ocean," and giant waves crashed toward me.

I honestly can't decide if this marvel is a good or bad thing. My immediate temptation would be to scoff at the need to reproduce electronically what we have access to naturally. My second reaction is to grieve at the society that is so far removed from nature that we must use electronic devices to simulate nature's sounds in order for us to get to sleep at night. But I will also admit to having a fair amount of guilty envy toward whoever thought to package and sell the things I have taken for granted for so many years. Whoever they are, they deserve to be making money, for they epitomize the essence of American commerce. I can even see the slogan: "Meeting your artificial health needs since 1993."

I wonder if the inventors of the sound simulator use their own product, or if they have made enough money that they've moved to the country or purchased homes by the ocean? It's an interesting conundrum. If you believe in your own product enough to sell it, will you also use it when the you have the resources to produce the sounds legitimately? And do you sleep well, knowing that your customers are getting to sleep using a product that is but a poor substitute for the original?

Ellen Rosewall

58

I may or may not ever come up with a product of any kind that will allow me to retire in luxury, but I know that whenever I go to Walloon I will always sleep well. Maybe it's the air, as my grandfather supposed. The air certainly does smell sweet – a combination of pine sap, wildflowers and rich, moist earth. Or then again, it could be the sounds of the lake, washing gently to shore or slapping lazily against the bottom of the boat.

I think I'll go take a nap.

Little Fishes...

When I was a child, my parents enrolled me in swimming lessons every summer. I started in the Pollywog class and worked my way through Tadpole and Frog. I don't remember the upper level classes. I am fairly certain that I didn't receive a bathing suit patch that read "Galapagos Tortoise." The rationale for the lessons was simple: to make us comfortable in the water so that we would be able to take care of ourselves at Walloon.

The swimming lessons accomplished much. They allowed me to develop a life-long love of swimming and a means of exercise that is now touted as an "aerobic, non-impact, total body workout." They allowed me to develop skill enough to participate in my only team sport ever (unless you count choir). They kept me outside in the summer, but out of trouble (most of the time). They didn't necessarily give me the tools I needed to stay safe and happy in Walloon Lake. That I think I would have accomplished anyway.

Our cottage abuts the lake in a place where a near-miracle has occurred: a sand bar extends out into the lake about 500 yards and then drops off sharply, in contrast to the gradually deepening water you find at most shorelines. The water is three to four feet deep all over our swimming area, floored by a fine sand bottom, no reeds or muck. What more do you need to make young children comfortable? We jumped right in when we were toddlers and haven't left since.

Since the water off our dock is so user-friendly, there's always someone there to play with. When Peter was about three, Charlie taught him to "swim" by carrying him on his back as far as the next dock. The water is nice and clear, so you can always play shark with unsuspecting old folks or search for clams. Nowadays, we like to play water frisbee or keepaway with a tennis ball. The water is shallow enough that you can move fairly quickly while still providing a little challenge for those who wish it.

We were in the water so much as kids that Dad once claimed that we were just like little fishes and moaned that one day we would wake up with gills. I really didn't see what would be wrong with that. In fact, turning into a fish might be the only way that I can accomplish my unfulfilled dream.

Those swimming lessons made me into a fairly accomplished swimmer. I swam in meets in junior high and high school and collected a manila envelope full of ribbons and certificates and even one trophy. I continued to swim into adulthood, at one point (when the Y was across from my office) lapping a mile a day. I can take care of myself. But I've never swum across the lake.

The lake is only a mile across where we live. It's relatively calm water, and although it's certainly much different than swimming laps

Ellen Rosewall

in a heated pool, it's never seemed an impossible task to me. Yet, I've never done it. I've been scared by stories of swimmers accidentally getting run over by power boats; by swimmers cramping and drowning; by stories of other cottagers, "real" swimmers, trying and failing.

Each year that passes and each pound of flesh that accumulates leads me further and further away from even thinking about swimming across the lake, yet I still do. It's a hard dream to give up.

Thunderstorms...

It's spring in Wisconsin as I write this, and last night we had our first thunderstorm of the season. I was awakened in the middle of the night by the familiar low rumbling of a storm several miles away, the kind you can't decide in the first moments of waking whether it's just a distant train or perhaps a semi-truck with the beginnings of a faulty muffler. I lay awake as long as I could, straining for the sound, even as the storm moved off. It's one of my favorite sounds.

It's a sound I missed desperately when we lived in California. I had not realized before living there that most of California does not get electrical storms. People who have lived in California all their lives have never felt the air pulled so taut it needs to be split by a slash of lightning. They've never watched bales of over-stuffed clouds roll over each other and pile higher and higher, growing dark and menacing until the anticipation is nearly unbearable. And they've never jumped at the first crack of thunder or sighed with relief at the start of the rainfall on rooftop, sidewalk and trees.

Watching a thunderstorm at the cottage is particularly satisfying. As the storm gathers above the lake, the wide skies afford a luxurious view of clouds filling the sky and lightning that extends for miles. The rain hits the lake with a "whooshing" sound and drips off the porch roof in counterpoint. We stay outside until the last possible moment, then watch from the sanctuary of the porch or the living room, depending on the wind.

When Steve (a lifelong California resident) married Jan and came to the cottage for the first time, we were on storm watch daily hoping that the skies over Walloon would put on a good show for him. We were not disappointed when, one afternoon, the clouds began to darken in the west. Steve rushed in and got his video camera and went down to the dock. The result is epic. With the camera trained on a bank of dark clouds, Steve is heard muttering, "oh, wow, oh, wow," like a 60s throwback, as the camera jerks from side to side every once in awhile trying to catch a lightning bolt. Behind him, Jan's voice says "Steve, it's time to go in now," with increasing urgency until the rain starts and it's not an option any more.

The exchange reminded me of a sign on a beach in California: "WARNING. The ocean can be DANGEROUS and can cause INJURY or DEATH. DO NOT turn your back on the ocean. DO NOT swim alone. Thank you for patronizing your state parks." It also reminded me that Peter, who spent grades one through three in California schools, was taught to duck and cover in case of earthquake, a skill that came in quite handy in October of 1989 but was of little use when we moved to Wisconsin and the first tornado siren went off.

From childhood, I've carried deep within me the Midwest version of beach warnings: ELECTRICAL STORMS can be DANGEROUS. DO NOT take a shower when there's lightning. DO NOT remain in the open. Yet I'm attracted to the elements like a dangerous liaison. Feeling the restlessness that comes with changing barometric pressure or a crack of thunder explode in the pit of your stomach is essential for people like me, who live isolated from the intimacy of nature for most of the year. It's so powerful, so scary-cool, that all I have to do is lie in bed and listen to a distant rumble to feel that connection again.

Oh, wow, oh wow.

A Boat is a Hole You Pour Money Into...

We don't buy new boats. As I've noted before, we don't have any particular desire to go fast, and we certainly don't feel the need to keep up with the Joneses (particularly since the Joneses moved to Texas in 1979), so we have for the most part avoided the dollars and effort expended by others in boat upkeep. With one notable exception.

Steve and Jan are sailors – real sailors, who have taken classes and crewed boats on San Francisco Bay. They purchased a dinghy sailboat for use at Walloon – a poor substitute for the 40-foot schooners they were used to, but the 40-footers weren't exactly within the Walloon budget. For a smaller boat, it was a beaut. It did have some problems, though. It sat low in the water, and had some cracks in the seal between top and bottom, so they knew some repair work would be necessary. Steve quickly took over the project, opening the big doors to the long unused boathouse and assembling his materials with a great sense of purpose.

The first discovery, once the boat was opened, was that the foam flotation material was completely waterlogged and needed to be replaced. The removal used at least a three-month's supply of the official trash bags issued to rural residents (causing Mom to have to go downtown and beg for more from an unsympathetic civil servant), but the cleaned out hull offered the exciting promise of getting to fill it with new flotation material: amazing stuff that when mixed with water, expanded to about 500 times its size. Waiting for the material to arrive was difficult, but Jan, Steve and Linda filled the time by sanding, scraping and prepping – at least, Steve sanded, scraped and prepped while Jan and Linda handed him supplies like surgical nurses.

The magic day arrived. Excitement mixed with fear that too much potion had been purchased and the stuff would expand to fill the boathouse, crushing observers between boat and wall. The three dutifully mixed and poured, and waited. And waited. Finally, when the flotation had expanded to about 1 and 1/1,542 times its original size, they called around to find more and discovered that it had been banned for being hazardous to the environment.

Not to be deterred, they finally located the last remaining bags of the acceptable substitute in the area and, although it didn't work much better, there was now enough flotation material in the boat to at least give it a try.

By this time the project had taken a full twelve days. The morning of their last day of vacation dawned bright and clear, and Steve worked furiously (fortified with drinks and snacks from nurses Jan and Linda) to seal the boat back up. Finally – success! The boat was launched with much flurry and taking of pictures. Steve took the first shakedown cruise, and was flushed with success until the two observers back on the dock noticed the mast leaning a bit to leeward. Steve managed to bring the boat back to shore just before the mast leaned so far askew that it snapped the hull in two. It seemed that the ancient flotation material had also anchored the mast to the bottom of the hull.

Jan thought Steve would be crushed. He had poured his entire vacation into putzing around with this boat, only to discover that they would have to begin again next year. With great sympathy, she put a comforting hand on his shoulder. When he turned around, his face was alight with joy. He would have to begin again next year!

DEAR LAKE ...

Dear lake,

You're really deep, you know that? Get it?

Love,

me

The Test...

We've been aware of The Test most of our lives. It is well known, discussed openly among natives, and passed down from generation to generation. It had not, to my knowledge, been publicly addressed until August 11, 1995, when Sarah Faulkman, crack reporter for the *Walloon Lake Villager,* published the following, which she claimed to have reconstructed from the "long-lost" Handbook of Walloon Lake Traditions:

"...whereby any Wallooner of marrying age which is considering Engagement to an Individual whose feet have never touched the shores of said Lake, must, by virtue of his or her Status as Wallooner and in the singular attempt to perform, as it were (in the manner of

The Princess and the Pea), the Ultimate Test in weighing the worth of the Marriage Candidate... must subtly bring the Candidate North to the very waters of said Lake, being careful to observe even the merest hints of Distaste or Disinterest in the part of the Candidate for Walloon. Intent that should those signs appear, the Relationship is to be immediately severed with no hope for reconciliation, and thenceforth the Wallooner's acknowledgment of the some-time Candidate is to be only an occasional curt nod in the Individual's general direction...

...special sanction is possible for those Marriage Candidates which the Wallooners feel display an uncommon dose of Good Taste and Sense, but which perhaps have had a tedious trip North and are feeling unusually Crabby upon their initial encounter of said Lake, or first arrival at night or in a fog, a downpour, a blizzard, or any other Unexpected Adverse Weather Condition which might hinder the Obvious Glory of Walloon, whereby those Candidates are to be given a few days' chance to become acquainted with the many Redeeming Qualities of said Lake, after which they will be subject to said Test..."

It is broadly assumed that the three men that currently are regular visitors to Ja-Ma-Ca by virtue of their marriage into our family, passed The Test. In fact, in the truest sense of the word, none of them did. By coincidence of time and distance, the first look that Charlie, Michael and Steve got at the cottage was after they were married to us, by which time, according to our measurement, it was too late. By then, it was a "love me, love my dock" kind of situation, and The Test was administered only as confirmation. Fortunately, but not unexpectedly, all of these wonderful men fell in love with Walloon the minute they stepped onto the property. Michael claims he had no choice, he was married to the lake immediately by virtue of losing his wedding ring on the second day of our honeymoon. Charlie, on the other hand, often says that had he been brought to Walloon prior to his marriage to Mom, she would never have really known why he married her. Which brings up another issue, one that I wish the *Walloon Lake Villager* would send Sarah or someone equally resourceful to investigate.

Mom has said more than once that she didn't know anyone who had failed The Test, but she did know a few marriages that wouldn't have taken place if the Intendeds hadn't been so enamored of Walloon. From the few instances we do know like that, it is not hard to imagine the next step: someone actively seeking out a Walloon family to marry into. The situation is so full of horrifying opportunity that it's beyond the realm of possibility that someone, somewhere, hasn't at least played with the idea.

Thank goodness the men who married the Wetherbee girls had no such dastardly intentions. We think.

Gimme That Old Time Religion...

For those who haven't been to church in awhile, the word Methodist might conjure images of old-timey summer tent revivals; of sweaty, white-shirted preachers waving tattered Bibles at the congregation while the women fanned themselves with woven straw fans and the men tried not to scratch under their shirt collars.

I grew up Methodist, and although the modern Methodist Church has very little to do with fire and brimstone (in most cases), I think that there must have been something preached subtly from the pulpit or whispered among the congregation that made us believe deep down in our souls that we would not be truly cleansed before we were washed in the sweat of a summertime camp meeting. Combine those secret emotions with the fact that a deep blue lake with clouds reflected in it tends to make one think of heaven, and you might come to the conclusion that northern Michigan just might be a good place for a religious colony. Guess what. It is.

The little town of Bay View is almost completely swallowed up by the city of Petoskey now, but in the late 1800s it was more isolated, a summer getaway for Methodist ministers and their flocks. Oh, they had to preach and teach, of course, they were Methodists after all and work ethic is one of those things that just couldn't be changed when fire and brimstone became politically incorrect. But preaching and teaching in graceful summer homes while gazing out over Little Traverse Bay and sharing ideas with other like-minded souls seemed just as good as a real vacation. And so, Bay View was born, the summer homes surrounding a campus of buildings that would grow to also serve, in the Chatauqua tradition, as a summer religious institute and music school. Even now, Bay View serves as a spiritual and cultural anchor for the community, providing not only a pleasant work vacation for ministers all over the world, but also church services, lectures, classes, recreational activities and musical performances for the residents of the surrounding area and tourists from all over the world.

Attending church at Bay View on Sunday mornings is always a treat. You have to park your car several blocks away because of the crowds and the winding, narrow streets, so you try not to soil your Sunday go-to-meeting shoes as you walk delicately toward the building, streams of people coming from all directions. You see ladies with cotton shirtwaist dresses in pinks and greens leading little girls with long curly hair in dresses with bows at the back. Gentlemen in summer sport coats hand hymnals to the arriving pilgrims. You enter and seek out a spot, in the center section only if you're lucky or early, and seat yourself on a fold-down auditorium chair.

The service takes place in the hall that also serves as the auditorium for musical recitals and theatrical performances, and it is generally packed. The walls are coated with generations of crisp white paint, and you can usually feel sand crunching beneath your feet on the concrete floor. It's not air conditioned, but if it gets too stuffy, one of the linen-jacketed gentlemen proceeds to the side to crank open a window. Every week is different, for every week they have invited a different guest preacher. You never know what you're going to get, but you know that chances are it will be good, for Bay View has built up enough of a reputation that they can afford to be picky. If the preacher is particularly inspirational, you can come back the next day or the next for the series of lectures scheduled during their week-long visit (see previous: work ethic).

After over forty years of going to services at Bay View, I can comfortably meet my maker with the knowledge that I have done my Methodist duty. I have sat in a crowded room on an uncomfortable seat in the summer time listening to a visiting preacher speak the word to me. I have sung the grand old hymns while hundreds of others raised their voices. I just won't mention that the experience didn't involve sweat or damning people to eternal flame. I won't let on how much I enjoyed it. And I most certainly won't tell St. Peter that we usually went to brunch at the Perry afterward.

Settling Down...

Michael is a college professor, and he hates the first few weeks of summer. During the year, he goes nonstop, slogging through the full teaching days, evening rehearsals and weekend performances that are the hallmark of a music teacher. All year, he longs for a minute of rest, yet when it comes, he says it's like putting the brakes on a runaway train.

Once, when I was in the midst of a busy and stressful time at work, I went for a day-long getaway to a state park on our (Wisconsin) side of Lake Michigan. I sat by the water, wondering why I wasn't relaxing, and then I noticed that my eyes were darting around, focusing on each wave, bird or cloud for only a millisecond before moving on. I figured that if my eyes were unable to settle down, my brain was probably continuing to send signals to the rest of my body at a dizzying pace. Even though my bare feet were cradled in sand and the sun was warming my face, I was getting no rest at all.

It's no secret that life on our planet is moving at a speed that is not only faster than any time in human history, but increasing exponentially by the day. When I was a child, our family was busy, but my heavens. These days, most everyone balances a life of job, family, and volunteer work, squeezing in social activities when time permits. And they "relax" by watching television, which throws images and messages at us at an incredible pace. No wonder we're all wound up tighter than cheap watches. No wonder our brains keep firing long after the stimulation ceases.

This essay is not meant to be a critique of modern society. I like modern society. I live here. Most of the time, it's fun and exciting, and there are lots of things to see and do and learn. It's just that, whenever I get wound a little too tightly, I am even more grateful for the presence of the cottage and Walloon Lake.

Vacationing at the cottage is very different from going to Disney World or the Grand Canyon. My body and brain have been trained for over forty years to respond to the unique stimuli of life at the lake. I've never done a scientific study, but I'm sure that after a day of sitting on the porch, dangling my feet in the water or walking down the back road my pulse slows, my muscles relax and I settle down. It's a conditioned response. I am confident that it would take a pretty unusual vacation to leave feeling as wound up as when I arrived.

"Settle down!" we tell children. It's an interesting phrase. Is that like a box of cereal, "contents may settle during shipping"? Do our bodies, taut as a string pulled tight, sag like that same string when released? What physical changes happen when we refresh and renew, and what changes do we need to seek in order to keep moving on our daily tightropes without falling? The original meaning of recreation, after all, means to create anew, to come back from our time away from our everyday lives restored to our original, whole selves.

I'm not a doctor, nor do I play one on TV. I'm probably treading on shaky ground by even raising these questions. All I know is what works for me, and that is a simple formula of one 100-year-old cottage, a cobalt blue lake, and a front porch with family sitting on it.

Fishers of None...

When we were young, we tried, we really did. Dad dutifully purchased an annual fishing license, and since we didn't want to waste it, we went out at least once per summer and gave it the old college try. We were spurred on by the knowledge that Walloon is reputed to be an excellent fishing lake, with small mouth bass, perch and lake trout in abundance.

We also knew that participation in all water sports, including fishing, is *de rigeur* for vacationing on a lake. So we put in our best effort. It seldom amounted to much, however, for two simple reasons. The first was to be expected for girls our age: we thought fishing was gross, since it involved putting in and removing hooks from living things. The second was probably even more significant: Mom hates fish, and refused to clean or cook our catches, meaning that any fishing expedition just ended with throwing things back into the lake any-way.

I do remember a couple of exceptions to this bleak participation record in America's favorite pastime. One involved our family friends and frequent cottage guests, the Colemans. Dick Coleman is a fisher and fish lover, and apparently didn't mind cleaning them, because I remember a perch dinner that was probably the only one ever served at the cottage, at least since Mom has been matriarch. However, I also remember that Dick Coleman taught me to put ginger snap cookies on the grill, making them soft, warm and mmm-mmm good. This memory is shared by absolutely no one else in the family, who swear I am imagining the great taste of grilled ginger snaps and accuse me, as I get older, of having increasingly frequent "ginger snap moments." So perhaps the table full of golden, crispy fried perch fillets fresh from the lake is also a figment of my imagination.

I cannot be accused of imagining the second incident, for it is recorded for posterity in our guest book. The guest book has also served upon occasion as a history log, and in 1967 is written, with appropriate pride, "this is the year we caught 28 fish in one day off the dock!" Apparently, we had even given up on going out in the boat by that time, and Dad figured since we were going to throw them back anyway, why put any effort into the project. But he did take a picture of the three of us with our proud trophy, twenty-eight small catches that we had strung on a line like real fishers, before the poor fish were freed to get on with their lives.

It's a shame, really. Apparently, according to the informative booklet put out by the Fisherman's Information Bureau, drop-offs like the one right in front of our cottage are prime places to fish. In the section entitled *Where to Fish: Lakes,* we learn that the minnows run in schools along the edge of the drop-off, aquatic insects hatch out of the gravel bottoms and swim toward the surface, and lake fish in great numbers lie in wait for these treats. In the early morning during the summer there is frequently a fishing boat sitting at the drop-off line about 500 feet from the end of our dock.

By this time, though, we realize it is no use. Fishing still involves the insertion and removal of hooks, and Mom still hates fish. These basic facts of life will never change, warm ginger snaps notwithstanding. But even though we are shamed by the fact that we are blatantly thumbing our noses at America's No. 1 Sport, we are somewhat consoled by the fact that enough other people love fishing to keep our favorite restaurants well stocked with plenty of whitefish, perch and lake trout. That's good enough for us.

Let's Put on a Show...

We sing, my husband and I. That's not generally considered one of the most viable ways to make a living ("Learn how to play the piano," growled my father, "and at least you can play in a bar."), and to be perfectly honest, we don't literally earn our keep just by singing. Michael is a choral conductor and teaches voice lessons. I do consulting work with singers, other musicians, choirs, theaters and museums, helping them raise money and market themselves. And we sing – when we're asked and when we can. I don't know about my husband, but I know my career choice was shaped at least in part by some of our childhood activities at the cottage.

I suppose most kids go through the "let's put on a show in the barn" stage. Our budding performing talents were encouraged by the fact that we had a couple of great "barns" at the cottage.

One was the archway separating the dining room from the living room. The audience sat comfortably, nursing their beers and iced teas, while the actors stored their costumes and props in the kitchen and made their grand entrance one by one into the dining room. These shows usually involved a number of little skits and songs, notable for their quantity rather than their quality. I remember one show that had a couple of showstoppers called "I Am Hot Man," followed immediately by "I Am Cold Woman." These did involve some method acting, however, and of course they were duly appreciated by the albeit prejudiced crowd.

Our best "barn" was the boathouse. More accurately, the roof of the boathouse, which extends out over the water and which we normally use for sunning, watching sunsets and picnics. When I was in my early teens our next door neighbors from home, the Dells, visited us at the cottage, and my best friend Carolyn and I spent most of our vacation together preparing for our big debut as the String Sisters. We hand made dozens of programs – probably operating on the "it's good, so people have *got* to come" theory that drives many of my clients even today. I still have at least ten of them, carefully typed and individually decorated, with the S's in "String" and "Sisters" cleverly shaped like guitars and treble clefs.

Carolyn and I played ukeleles. For most people, the popularity of the uke had died out when flappers went out of style. But some mutant strain had survived into the early 60s, and somehow we not only got our hands on two instruments, but learned quite a few chords on them. We rehearsed for hours and hours, proud of our intricate renditions and soulful harmonies. The big evening came, and we thrilled the appreciative crowd with folk songs and Beatles tunes. We had just a few programs left over. But everyone in attendance agreed that the setting, with the sun sparkling on the lake behind us, couldn't be beat.

I still sing, whenever I can. But I also talk. One of the things I do (that people don't always pay me for) is to travel around the country, giving speeches, talking to legislators and meeting people, trying to convince everyone I talk to that music belongs in our schools and the arts belong in our communities. I do this because I want to make sure that in the future, whenever a couple of little girls or a bunch of big people want to put on a show in a barn or on a boathouse, in a living room or classroom, park or performing arts center, they can do it. And that people will know enough to teach them, to encourage them, and to make sure there are no programs left over.

Porch Sitting...

According to movies and television, people used to sit on front porches a lot. I don't know if they really did. Sometimes we tend to "remember" what life was like in the earlier part of this century with great nostalgia, when in fact our fantasies had more resemblance to a Norman Rockwell painting than real life. Recently, however, I've started to hear praises to the front porch sung more and more frequently.

A management consultant I know refers to the process of getting to know a new client as "porch sitting," meaning that by visiting with a client over coffee and chatting about families, current events and hobbies, you can get to know far more about the problem they'd like you to solve than if you spend hours in a conference room with flip charts and erasable markers. I also know a sociologist who claims that

America's problems would be solved if we allowed ourselves to return to the metaphorical front porch, a place where we could feel the breeze on our face and a connection to our neighbors.

I think it's a great idea. Front porches, whether metaphorical or real, are good for lots of cool stuff. Instead of sitting inside a stuffy house on a summer's evening, you take a lemonade or iced tea to the front porch and relax, catching up on the evening newspaper or doing a crossword puzzle. It has to be a front porch, though, because an essential part of the experience is watching neighbors walk by, checking out who is painting their soffits or putting in a fence, and seeing which car is parked in whose driveway.

The electronic media has also shown us that couples used to court on front porches. I'm not sure about that one. Unless you're sitting on the Walton's front porch with the next neighbor seven or eight miles down the mountain, the potential presence of the prying eyes of the neighbors would tend to negate any privacy gained away from family members.

Today, we have decks and patios, but they serve a different function. They are purposely placed by the back door, and are surrounded by foliage for privacy. Decks are social, too, but not in the same way. You feel as though you need matching furniture on a deck. Guests who join you on a deck are invited. I can't imagine pushing aside the Sunday paper so a guest could find a seat on a deck.

I can afford to be picky, though, because our cottage has one of the all-time great front porches. It is so beautiful and stately that it defines the entire cottage. It's nice and wide, and has a wooden railing around three sides, except where the magnificent stairs descend to the lawn. There's usually at least one beach towel or swim suit draped over the railing, which is also conveniently wide enough for drinks. There's a swing hanging from one side, and rolled-up blinds (which I refuse to roll down – see Bats, p. 37). A variety of chairs, ranging from ancient wicker to wooden rockers to department store folding chairs are lined up facing the water. The space behind the chairs is home to air mattresses, water shoes, and other water implements that because of the water or sand they carry are not welcome in the house. There are usually a couple of dead June bugs by the screen door, martyred in the vain attempt to seek the light inside the cottage the previous evening.

In the summertime, the front porch is our base of operations. Important tasks are accomplished here, from plotting the day's activities to working together on crossword puzzles to solving our little problems and the world's. You can be by yourself on the front porch, or you can be with someone else. It's up to you, and there's no pressure.

Of course, our front porch at the cottage fulfills that old-time social function as well. More often than not, a neighbor will stroll down and join us on the porch after dinner. It's also a situation without pressure. You can visit when you feel like it and not make your hosts feel like they have to serve you something, although it's a great excuse to get out the brownies. You can leave just as easily, without any worry about social graces or outstaying your welcome. Everyone understands.

I never courted on this front porch, although one summer I did hang out with some older kids who liked to meet around a campfire on our neighbor's beach. There was a boy who walked me home one night, and I thought he was going to kiss me, but Dad appeared at the screen door and that was that. I suppose the closest I've come to courting on the porch was holding hands with Michael, but only after we were married. We did take our honeymoon at the cottage, and we were alone, so it's fair to assume that some kissing went on. I suppose that counts.

SPARKLE ISLAND

Finally, our front porch admirably fulfills the most important porch function, that of nosiness. From the vantage point of our front porch you can see onto the front porches of several neighbors, check out who is painting their boathouse or who has let their geraniums go, and see which boat is pulled up to whose dock.

Not bad for a metaphor.

Peter and the Amazing Traveling Playpen...

When Peter was almost eleven months old, he made his first trip to the cottage, and we were faced with the dilemma of how to keep him safe and reasonably contained while we had the leisure to enjoy our vacation. I envy parents now who have these wonderful portable playpens you can fold up into a nylon sack the size of a sleeping bag, but we didn't have that option, and the regular playpen was too big to fit in the car, so off we went in to town to try to find something that would fit the bill.

Incredibly, we found something that was just perfect. It was like a little corral: a series of panels that could be bent into a modified circle or square to enclose the baby. You could secure the open sides together, but there was no bottom, so the baby could feel his feet in the grass or sand between his toes. It could be folded up and carried like a lawn chair. It was such a wonderful invention that Mom bought it herself, certain that it would accommodate generations of babies from here to everlasting.

For many babies, the corral was probably just the ticket. But Peter at this age was already adept at trotting around while hanging on to coffee tables and sofa cushions, and he had never liked being imprisoned in a playpen out of reach of the real action. When we placed him in the corral, he promptly crawled over, pulled himself up on the metal bar at the top of one of the panels, picked it up and started scooting it toward where he wanted to be. By the time we looked up from our novels, he was halfway out the door, dragging the 4-foot diameter corral with him.

Tired parents who want a few minutes rest on vacation are not easily deterred. We tried lashing one side of the corral to the posts on the fence around the boathouse deck, figuring that he couldn't move it far enough to cause any danger, and we could still relax in the sun. That was a dream that lasted about ten minutes, as Peter promptly walked the corral to the edge of the boathouse, nearly dropping down the hill to the dock in the process.

We tried many configurations of the magic corral, but Peter has always had a one-track mind, and this was a baby who a few months later would be able to sneak downstairs and turn on the television even after we had closed the door with a washrag in it and smeared the doorknob with vasoline™. Thankfully, Aunt Linda was there, and she was just in the process of deciding to leave her health administration job and go back to school to become a pediatric nurse. Peter was in the right place at the right time for Linda's pent-up nurturing skills, so as Michael and I watched gratefully, Linda, good sport that she is, climbed into the corral and sat down among the blocks and boats. It didn't matter to Peter that we had gotten the corral for the purpose of enclosing him *away* from adults. He was happy at last.

I don't know what happened to the corral. It disappeared after that summer. That's okay, because I, for some reason, didn't get around to supplying any more babies to play in it, and now there are an amazing number of Good Housekeeping™-sealed marvels for young parents to try. My only regret is that Peter won't some day have the opportunity to try to get a few moments vacation while his babies walk away with the playpen.

DEAR LAKE...

Dear lake,

The good part is saying hello to you at the beginning of our time at the cottage. The hard part is saying goodbye at the end. The last time I saw you, I stayed on the dock for a long time, memorizing every detail, every sound and smell.

Now I'm most of a country away from you and there's nothing here to help me remember. Once, in search of you, I went to a place they called a lake, but it was red from the clay, with rings around the edges to show how the lake had shrunk during the long drought. And still there were people all over...in the lake on their boats, by the side of the lake on blankets or with volleyball nets, cars spilling out beyond the parking lot onto the adjoining grass.

When I first came to visit here, I felt very uncomfortable, because the natural world was so different. I didn't know the names of the trees or the flowers, and the ground was covered with golden stubble instead of green grass. I've traveled a lot, to the east and west and south and even across the ocean, but traveling is different than living and I found out that knowing what the earth is doing and how the seasons react centers me in such a fundamental way that I never noticed it before. Now, I have fallen in love with eucalyptus bark underfoot as I walk, redwood trees that carry the wisdom of hundreds of years and the way the clouds gather above the foothills at the end of Page Mill road. But the smell of white pine, the song of goldfinches and the icy blue-green of a glacial lake is by now programmed into my genetic memory, and I know I must see it soon or lose a part of myself.

Who knows where my life will take me when we leave here? The only thing I know is that somehow, the road will, must, lead back to you.

Love,

me

Rituals...

When you look in the dictionary for the meaning of ritual, you will find two distinct definitions. The first associates ritual with religious practice: a ceremony or sacred rite. The second asserts that any activity, if performed frequently enough, becomes a ritual. That second definition bothers me, because I think we've become careless with the use of the word "ritual," using it to define things like watching soap operas, which should more accurately be called bad habits.

I think of ritual as an activity performed frequently, faithfully, and lovingly enough so that over time the performing of the activity becomes embued with meaning beyond itself. It becomes a sacred act, and we seek to continue doing it not just because it's that time of day or because we've always done so, but because doing it gives us some spiritual food.

Going to the cottage has been one of the few constants in lives that have filled with moving from home to home and even from state to state, with marriages begun and ended, with ever changing daily tasks of school, home and job. Over that length of time, we have amassed a great number of rituals. Many we acknowledge, many we just perform without thinking. All have added to the sacredness of our life there.

The first rituals on the agenda are arrival rituals. Immediately after getting out of the car, before even going into the cottage, we must go down and say hello to the lake. Some of us insist on touching the lake with fingers or toes; others find enough meaning in simply standing quietly for a few minutes and absorbing the looks, sounds and smells. Amid the flurry of hugging and greeting, we also find the time to wander throughout the cottage, touching things that have been there for awhile and remarking on any new addition. We sneak a peek at the corner cabinet to be sure there are gumdrops in the candy dish, and touch the Petoskey stones on top of the bookshelf. I'm not sure this is universal, but no matter which bedroom I'm unpacking in, I need to go to one of the front bedrooms to hear the sound of the waves hitting the shore through the window.

While at the cottage, there are certain things that must be done before you leave. I feel confident that these activities meet my definition of ritual, for they accomplish a wonderful purpose of creating shared memories and that elusive "quality family time." These activities include going for planked whitefish at Juillerets (except for Mom, who always gets the hamburger club), reading the guest book (actually there are three now, one on top of the other on the phone table, dating back to 1948), and lighting a fire in the fireplace at least once, no matter how hot it is.

There are many rituals which involve field trips: to the pier at Harbor Springs to gaze longingly at the yachts, to the drawbridge in

Ellen Rosewall

downtown Charlevoix, to some of our favorite Petoskey shops, like Games Imported, Symon's General Store and of course the wonderful bookstores. Many of our rituals, like sacred rites throughout history, involve food: Kilwin's ice cream, Hinckley's sweet corn and American Spoon Foods.

The saddest rituals come at the time we have to leave. Rituals of gathering possessions from the various parts of cottage, porch and dock and loading up the car provide (in modern parlance) closure, but that doesn't mean we have to like them. These rituals are usually lengthy, interrupted frequently by "one last" game of Boggle or look at the guest book.

When we've come full circle, we return to the lake for the final ritual. Gazing out over the water, we try to gather enough of the lake inside of our soul to last throughout the winter. We turn and look up the hill at the cottage, memorizing each detail. Sometimes we touch the water one last time, and if it's sunny, the lake seems to wink at us, telling us not to take the parting so seriously. We do anyway.

Cherries to the Left of Me...

I'm not sure why different crops flourish in different areas of the country. Grandpa Charlie could tell you – he was a farmer for many years and then became a banker and made loans to farmers for another many years. One of his favorite pastimes even now is driving through the countryside at a pace and direction that the uninitiated would call "aimless wandering," but which is in fact a studied examination of the various farms along the route (on a recent trip to Green Bay, he told me grandly that "you have the best dairy area in the country." I didn't know whether to be flattered or shocked, until I realized he was talking about cows).

Whether you are wandering aimlessly or really going somewhere, if you are driving anywhere in the area between Grand Traverse Bay and Little Traverse Bay you won't be able to miss the fact that you're in Cherry Country (the "best cherry area"?). Like I said, I can't tell you why. Not being a farmer, my guess would be that it has something to do with sandy soil, cool spring weather and the direction of the breeze off the lake. But other places have similar conditions and, with the exception of Door County, Wisconsin, directly across Lake Michigan on the opposite shore, they have not had the success with cherries that the Traverse area has.

For about three weeks in July, the cherries are at their peak. It is then that you see fruit stands every few miles along Highway 31 advertising "washed sweet" cherries. These are the cherries that seem to be in demand, but my favorites are the Montmorency, big tart cherries that are great in pie or dried to put in salads or eat like raisins. You can get some magnificent cherries during high season, but if you're not in Michigan in July, no matter – you'll find cherries year round in restaurants and on store shelves in everything from chicken salad to chutney.

Since during my childhood we normally came in August, I usually missed cherry season. But recently I had a chance to go to one of the "U-Pick-Em" cherry farms and fill my metal pail with fruit right off the tree. I hadn't realized until then that cherry picking is a very sensual experience. It is best when the sun is bright and high in the sky, beating down on your back as you walk through the field past the picked-over trees to get to a good one. You walk deep into the orchard and know you're close when you sense excitement by other pickers a few trees away.   Then you see it – a whole row of trees as yet untouched by human hands.   The branches are so heavy with fruit they bend close to the earth, the bright red of the cherries in sharp contrast to the green leaves. The ripe cherries come off in your hand with just a gentle tug, making a little "pop" as they pull away from the stem. After a few handfuls, your fingers become sticky with juice, and you can't resist slipping a fat cherry into your mouth. Surprise – it is

Ellen Rosewall

warm, and you realize that you have never before tasted a cherry that hasn't been stored in the refrigerator before eating. So you let the whole cherry linger a bit, getting used to your mouth, and slowly you half bite, half suck it, letting the juice explode deliciously in your mouth and rolling your tongue over the pit to get the last little bits of pulp. If you try hard enough, you can linger in the orchard for a good hour or more, even though it only takes a few minutes to fill up a pail when the pickin's good.

The romantic haze continued for Michael and me as we walked back to the barn, emptied our pails into coolers and plastic bags for the journey home, rinsed off our pails and our hands, and sat in the sun for a few minutes waiting for the rest to return from the fields. It lingered on the drive home, as we imagined the gourmet delights we would try with our bountiful treasure. We drooled at the thought of freezers full of pie, pantries full of jam and zippered plastic bags full of dried cherries. We thought we might experiment with new sauces and breads, cobblers and candies...after all, we had enough cherries to last us until December.

Then we got home, and spent nearly four hours pitting the damn things by hand.

Jesus Wants Me for a Sunbeam...

There is an ancient, dusty record player that has been sitting in the back bedroom since I was a child. Beside it is a wire rack that holds about five records. These are the only records, to my knowledge, that have ever been played on this record player. For some reason, we didn't think to bring up our own records when we were children, which was probably more Mom's decision than ours. The lack of variety didn't bother us because we are never inside for long periods of time anyway. Instead, we played the records over and over and over again, until they grew dear and familiar, only giving up their exalted position as our favorite electronic entertainment when we were teenagers and top 40 radio became more important. The records and record player remained, however, slowly gathering dust underneath the bed. I was tempted to get it out and try it a few years ago for old time's sake, but I was afraid of what would happen to the records and/or the electrical wiring, so there it sat.

I don't really need to hear the songs again, however, for the number of times I listened to them has made them a part of my permanent memory. We still sing together the song recorded by the Texas Christian Children's Choir, "Let the Sunshine In":

> Oh, let the sun shine in, face it with a grin.
> Smilers never lose, and frowners never win
> So let the sun shine in, face it with a grin
> Open up your heart and let the sun shine in.

The other side, "Jesus Wants Me for a Sunbeam," was a little more difficult to sing, as the melody contained a rather large skip upward on the word "beam" which usually involved a bit of squeaking. We usually just sing the first line and let it go at that.

This essay started out to be a memoir of some treasured childhood playthings, but now it is turning into something else, for I just now noticed (I'm only 45 years old, after all, you don't need to hit me over the head) that both sides of this record contained songs about the sun. That's some pretty clever symmetry on the part of the Texas Christian Children's Choir – a fact which I will acknowledge even though I never actually noticed it before. It also increases its worth as entertainment for good Christian parents at summer cottages: little children bask in the warm glow of the sun by day, and then curl up in their beach towels and listen to singable songs about the spiritual values of sunshine.

As an educator turned marketing professional, I am constantly seeking symbolism that will subtly educate my intended patron as well as entice them to purchase whatever I'm selling. We all know this happens all the time, whether we like it or not. Now, I have uncovered awesome evidence of just how powerful these subtle messages can be. I have, to use the jargon, internalized a wonderfully positive message. Trouble is, I am not at all sure it's the message the backers of the Texas Christian Children's Choir intended.

Over the years, I have indeed opened up my heart, and I've let the sun shine in. I've seen God in that sun, as I've seen God in the depths of the lake, the song of the bird and the sweet smell of the trees. I have known throughout my life that if I was troubled, or afraid, I could find God by feeling the warmth of the sun's rays surround me like a father's love, letting the water hold me like a mother's arms, or feeling the breeze caress me like a loving spirit. In these confusing times, some people who say that they're from the same religious family I claim have trouble with those thoughts. Perhaps the members of the Texas Christian Children's Choir, now all grown up, would be horrified if they knew how I had interpreted their message. Or perhaps they listened to the song often enough that they, too, were able to let the sun shine in.

The Story of the Long Legs...

In the woods of Northern Michigan, by the waters of Walloon, there lived a Long Leg, son of many generations of Daddy Long Legs and Grandaddy Long Legs. This Long Leg saw his plain, gray body and his long, gangly legs and was dissatisfied. He watched Goldfinch with his bright yellow body, Perch who shimmered as he swam, and Kingfisher with his majestic blue coloring. Long Legs envied the bright colors given to his brothers and sisters in nature, and wanted to be as colorful and beautiful as they.

Long Legs asked his mother why the Long Legs were cursed with such plainness. His mother replied with a story.

"Listen my child, and you shall hear," she began. "In the days of long ago, the days so ancient that the animal called jet-ski had not yet begun to roam the earth and part the waters with his mighty roar, there lived in the big house three little two-legged girls who were called Jane, Mary, and Carolyn, for such is the way of humans.

"The little girls heard the cry of the Long Legs, for your ancestors too longed to be colorful and beautiful, and in the ancient times they could communicate their wishes to their human sisters and brothers.

"So the little girls brought out of the big house pots filled with magic colors, and they gently brushed them on the backs of many Long Legs, and the Long Legs proudly strutted with their beautiful new bodies colored red and green and yellow.

"Now there was one Long Legs that had been off in the woods when the girls used their magic colors. He arrived home to see his beautiful brothers and sisters. 'Come look at us!' they said. 'We are so beautiful!' And their pride was so great that the plain Long Legs was ashamed, and went away.

After the sun had gone down and come up again, your great-grandaddy Long Legs came back, to try and find out how he could become beautiful, too. But when he arrived, he saw a horrible sight – all of the beautiful, colorful Long Legs lay dead.

"So, my son, you can see what happens to Long Legs when they give in to their pride. And now you know why, ever since, Long Legs have been content to be just the way they are."

Just the Girls...

It seemed like an ordinary gathering. Three women, who during the week filed patient charts, took X-rays and billed insurance companies had decided to take some time off and have fun together. They drove north on a beautiful fall weekend, ending up at Mary's cottage. For three days, they walked along the back road together, admired the colors of the changing leaves across the lake, played silly games, wrote in the guest book and laughed until their sides hurt. No big deal.

I'm sure even my Mom didn't think of that weekend as a reward for a long and courageous journey. Mom has always taken what life has put in front of her and dealt with it as it came. In fact, stubbornness in the face of adversity is so much a part of our family that we even have a joke about it. It seems that when Mom's twin,

Jane, was a little girl, my grandmother tried to elicit better behavior by warning her that if she was bad, Santa would put nothing but rotten potatoes in her stocking on Christmas Eve. "I don't care," said stubborn Jane. "I like rotten sotatoes, and all I want in my stocking is rotten sotatoes." Life has dealt Mom some rotten sotatoes, but she has usually found a way to live with them, even if she didn't always claim to like them all that much. Unlike Jane, Mom would probably take a look at the potatoes, size up the situation, figure that it could be worse, look, here's a couple that have some good left, and start looking through cookbooks trying to figure out a way to fix them.

At some point during my childhood, Mom realized that her marriage was not going to be the happy partnership she imagined it would be. During my adolescence and early adulthood she faced the joint traumas of my father's illness and my choice to rebel against conditions at home by leaving and leading a life she didn't understand. Her response to all of that was simply to love us all a little harder. After all, she would say later, she had to supply enough love for two parents. She also found herself a single mother at age forty-eight, with the need to reenter the workforce when her only job for twenty years had been raising a family.

The summer after my father died my mother used the cottage as a place to retreat and figure out what to do with the rest of her life. One of the leftover little rotten sotatoes in that situation was the fear of competing with younger workers who had grown up with modern office equipment. So she decided to volunteer at church, figuring they would cut her a little slack as she learned how to work the electric typewriters and copy machines. Of course, it didn't take long until she was office manager in a doctor's office, supervising a staff of five, including the doctor (who needed the most care of all). Not surprisingly with my Mom as supervisor, the office staff became like family, and so it was only natural that eventually they would end up on a weekend at Walloon. And just like all of our extended family, they fell in love with Ja-Ma-Ca as soon as they drove into the petanque court.

When my mother was young, she didn't imagine that she would someday invite coworkers to the cottage for a Girls Weekend Out. She didn't think that at age 55 she would even have coworkers. But there she was. I hope she had as much fun that weekend as she deserved to have.

DEAR LAKE

...

Dear Lake,

What do you look like in the winter? Having lived most of my adult life in the upper Midwest, it's not hard to picture. I suppose downtown Petoskey looks a little like Green Bay during the winter – snow pushed to the side of the road by snowplows and dirtied by the passing cars, skies uniformly gray instead of filled with the cumulus clouds of summer, cars streaked with salt residue.

I've lived almost a half century with you as a central part of my life, and yet I've never seen you before June or past September. It seems strange now that I think of it...even though there is a whole part of you I've never met, I feel as though our relationship is complete. In a way I'm like the mistress who only sees her lover under the most romantic of circumstances and doesn't have to be treated to the sight of her fair one emerging from bed in the morning.

Perhaps it is just as well that I don't lose the romance by seeing you during the winter, because sometimes when I wake up in the middle of the night, instead of imagining you as I know you to get back to sleep, I imagine what you must look like in the winter. The first thing I notice is how quiet it is. There are no boats, or swimmers splashing, and few cars go by on the back road. I imagine myself walking from quiet room to quiet room, perhaps wrapped in a quilt, just listening to the quiet. There is a fire in the fireplace, and I can see its reflection in the picture window in the living room as I gaze out over you. The bare trees reveal some things hidden in the lush summer: swingsets and the outlines of houses, but the thick blanket of snow has covered other things I'm used to seeing, so that the final effect is a reversal of image. The snow has even blurred the edges between the shore and the water, so that across the lake I can't even tell where you begin.

As I stand by the window, I realize that I'm not really looking at you – I'm looking at the snow covering you. Then, I notice a small black dot in the center of you – an ice fisher waiting patiently for a smallmouth bass to swim by. I imagine the fisher drilling through the ice to the water, and I imagine the fish swimming, more slowly than in summer, toward the bottom of the water where they live until enticed to the surface by a tasty treat on a hook. Underneath the snow, underneath the ice, you are still there.

It's February, and I'm covered with a layer of winter, too. But soon, the ice will slowly melt away, and our summer selves will be revealed, and we'll be together again.

Love,

me

Ellen Rosewall

The Murphy Desk...

Right by the back door, there is a marvelous invention that I've never seen anywhere else. I call it the "Murphy Desk," because it is similar to those like-named beds which fold into the wall when not in use. It was undoubtedly handmade, although I don't know whether it was created when the cottage was built or came later. When closed, it is barely noticeable. When open, it contains an array of information, office supplies and accessories that boggles the mind.

One of the best features of the Murphy Desk is that the writing surface is covered with a big green ink blotter, held in place at the four corners with four identical green thumbtacks. In addition to providing a cushioned surface which lends an air of elegance to the postcards you're writing to friends back home, the blotter is the absolute world's best surface for playing solitaire.

The cards stay put and they can be picked up and moved with ease. All you have to do is avoid the thumbtacks, which is easy, because they haven't been replaced in my lifetime and so are pretty much a part of the desk surface.

The shelves and cubbyholes of the Murphy Desk contain a mini-history of our life there. In addition to the things you'd expect, like postcards, stamps, pens and scissors, there is a postal scale on which a one-ounce letter costs fifteen cents, an assortment of batteries and various kinds of tape, and an old remote control to a television that has long since vanished. There is a nice variety of writing paper and stationary, a labelmaker that to my knowledge has never labeled anything, and, for some reason, an enema box. I've never asked; I don't want to know.

In the center of the storage area, there is an impressive stack of maps and brochures for areas and attractions throughout northern Michigan. The pile of information was ostensibly for renters, although we don't rent any more except to people who know the area as well as we do. We keep it because we love maps and brochures in our family. Collecting new ones wherever we go not only adds to our collection, it gives us an excuse at least once a year to go through the old ones "just to make sure there are no duplicates," and to plan new adventures. Over the years, it has also become a repository for selected articles that might shed light on the features or history of the area. I learned, for instance, that the bridge at Charlevoix is not a drawbridge (which lifts at one edge), but a bascule bridge, lifting in the middle. It's an important thing to know.

One of the family treasures in the Murphy Desk is a picture postcard which was taken from our boathouse by my Uncle Allen McGinnis, who lived next door. It came out in the 60s, and it's blurry and poor quality by today's photographic standards, but we still think it's one of the best pictures ever put on a postcard, and we've said so on the back of the postcard just so no guest will use it accidentally. They don't sell many postcards of Walloon Lake any more. Perhaps that is because most of the land is now private and if pictures were taken, permissions and royalties would probably be involved. Most of the postcards we see are of public places in Petoskey and around Little Traverse Bay, which are okay, but don't really convey a sense of where we are to our friends back home.

Over the years I've wondered why I've never seen another Murphy Desk. It seems like such a good idea. Then again, perhaps it's only a good idea because it fits so well right where it is.

Proof that People are Good...

Most people who follow college football with any kind of intensity are aware of the rivalry between Ohio State University and the University of Michigan. Over the years, especially when the teams are both toward the top of the rankings, the football teams have tended to serve as metaphors for the states themselves. It's a rivalry I've lived with pretty intimately all my life, having grown up in Columbus, Ohio (only a few miles from Ohio Stadium) and summering in Michigan (thankfully removed by a couple hundred miles of pine forest from Ann Arbor).

My grandfather was an attorney who was born and grew up in Columbus, possessed three degrees (two earned and one honorary) from Ohio State and was the Director of OSU's Development Fund for more than twenty years. You might say he was a fan. Over the years, due

SPARKLE ISLAND

in no small part to Grandfather's influence, my grandmother, most aunts and uncles, many cousins and of course all of my immediate family including me, my two sisters, Mom and Dad, became OSU grads as well. In fact, I remember my Grandfather's sense of betrayal when I announced my desire to attend the University of Minnesota for graduate school. It probably wouldn't have been so bad if it had not been another Big Ten school, but I suspect that I was allowed to go because Minnesota wasn't doing all that great in football right about then.

Yes, I was a bit of a rebel in those days, and I committed another major transgression by scheduling my wedding for the day of the Ohio State-Michigan game in 1978. Silly me, I just thought it was Thanksgiving weekend and therefore an opportunity for out-of-towners to attend more easily, but it turned out to be my mother's year in the ticket lottery rotation. Thank heaven Grandfather wasn't still around to see that. The wedding went on as scheduled (and is still going strong over twenty years later), but there was a bit of sneaking into the church kitchen to keep abreast of the score.

Since most of the summer residents of Walloon Lake have migrated northward from as close as Ann Arbor and as far south as Columbus and Cincinnati, it should come as no surprise that its shores contain ample evidence that the OSU-Michigan rivalry does not take a summer vacation. A surprising number of docks and boards proudly display their college flags, many of them flying their colors above the Stars and Stripes. The owner of a gas station in town even writes "Go Blue!" on the charge receipts of the cars that come in with Ohio license plates. We of course have the cottage discreetly decorated with OSU memorabilia, but we've never been showy about it. Not like some people.

With this history in mind, I'm sure you agree it was more than a little ironic that when the carburetor on our boat bit the dust on a

Ellen Rosewall

sunny July day, it did so right in front of Camp Michigania, which, as might be guessed, is a camp and retreat center owned by the University of Michigan for the pleasure of their faculty, alumni and other hangers-on. It sports the biggest blue flag with the gaudiest gold "M" on the entire lake. And no, we were not spying.

As we tried again and again to start the boat and be as unobtrusive as possible, we heard a cry from the shore: "Ahoy the pontoon! Are you in trouble?"   Before long, two strapping, tan young lads, obviously destined for greatness despite their choice of school, were towing our boat across the lake toward Ja-Ma-Ca. During the ride, we whispered that it was just a darn good thing that we didn't have a flag hanging on the boat or on our dock or we might not have gotten a ride.

It wasn't until we secured the boat and started up toward the cottage that we noticed that Mom was wearing her Ohio State sweatshirt.

Cheap Thrills...

Tourism is big business these days, and it's always been the major share of the economy of northern Michigan. Over the years, we've seen the area grow, new houses, motels and restaurants emerge, and the marketing get more and more sophisticated. We've been very lucky that we haven't also had to watch the erection of mega malls, chain restaurants owned by movie stars, water parks and other so-called tourist attractions that have invaded some other vacation areas like parasites.

Oh, you can drop some serious cash in Petoskey, Charlevoix and environs, but for the most part you will be dropping it in locally-owned restaurants, unique shops, and art galleries filled with the work of local painters and sculptors. And even though those activities are well worth the cost, we've never had the kind of money that would enable us to be among the tony crowd and linger (very long) in the stores that have "New York - Paris - Petoskey" painted on the front.

We've always found ways to take advantage of our time in northern Michigan while spending very little money. There's lots to do. Of course, the easiest are the pleasures of staying at home: swimming, reading a book in the sun, or taking a long leisurely float-boat ride and staring at houses. But even dreary days are fun, because then we have the excuse to go into town, have lunch at one of our favorite spots and walk the streets of Petoskey, gazing into the store windows. One of our favorite things is to go to the pier at Harbor Springs and walk up and down the docks, acting oh-so-very-nonchalant as we pass by the big yachts. Cost: $1.25 for the ice cream cone needed to give us an alibi.

When Mom was little, her mother would give each of the girls a dollar and send them off to the Emmet County Fair in early August. This dollar lasted the whole day, including a walk to Wimpy's Hamburger Stand just down the street. We haven't had the same kind of luck at the Fair, though. One summer when I was about ten, Dad played a carny game and won what I now realize was a totally horrible gold-tone horse with a gaudy clock in its stomach. Being of the age where horses were the center of my being, I fell in love immediately, which meant that Dad needed to spend about $50 more trying to win something equally wonderful for Linda. After that year, the budget didn't allow many more trips to the Emmet County Fair. Judging by the annual crowds, though, it looks like they're doing just fine without us.

Even though we can find Petoskey stones on our little beach and by the side of the road near the cottage, no summer is complete without a trip to what we call the Petoskey Stone Beach, near Nine Mile Point just south of Petoskey. The "beach" is actually covered with small rocks, and we've seldom walked there without finding a really good specimen. Even if we don't, the view over Little Traverse Bay is worth the excursion.

And speaking of Little Traverse Bay, that alone offers an endless variety of delights. Some evenings on our ice cream walks, we walk out on Sunset Beach and watch a glorious sunset. You can watch the sailboats on a sunny day, or take the high road in Harbor Springs for an even more spectacular view. We always watch for Beaver Island, which you can see on the horizon if the weather is just right. But the most fun of all is gasping when we clear the last hill going into town and see the Bay for the first time each day. Just like the lake, it is always different, always beautiful, and always awe-inspiring.

The preceding comments are offered as a public service to any tourists who want to experience what the locals do. Although if you should decide to become a tourist, you needn't worry about many traps. Other than the lake, the sky, the bay, the pines and the sunsets, that is.

Welcome Matthew...

Over the years, we have introduced many family members to the cottage. But we have waited a long, long time for Matthew to come and it will be a special pleasure to be there when he arrives.

I don't know the reasons why Matthew took his time finding Jan and Steve. Perhaps there was a long waiting list in heaven, perhaps certain things had to be just right for him to be able to leave whatever important angel work he was doing. I do hope his delayed arrival doesn't mean he will be late all his life, because Jan and Steve have a lot of catching up to do with him. They've been storing up things to show him for a very long time.

A few years ago, when Jan and Steve decided to start looking for Matthew, they wrote an open letter to potential birthmothers that said, in part: "One day, while watching our nephew laugh and play in the lake, we knew for sure the time was right for us to bring a new baby into our lives so we could share all of the special joys of Ja-Ma-Ca as a family." Peter was very proud of that, and immediately decided that it would be his job to teach the new baby to swim – perhaps carrying his nephew or niece on his back the way Grandpa Charlie had done with Peter when he was little.

For a long time, there was no reply to their letter. Then, a response came, but it had an unexpected, tragic result. The woman who answered was not a potential birthmother at all, but a clever con artist skilled at preying on vulnerable childless couples and running away to Mexico with their money. Jan and Steve cried a lot, then went to the television stations and the authorities and worked to make sure that no other couples would be victimized. In the process, they found at least twenty-six couples who already had.

Not long after all of this, Jan and Steve came to the cottage to begin healing and start the search all over again. One day, Jan and I were sitting in the living room and she plugged in her laptop computer. "Listen to this," she said, and she read me an e-mail which began, "My beautiful eighteen year old daughter is pregnant..."

I had a strong feeling even then that this e-mail was the beginning of the end of the journey, but all of us worked hard to keep hold of our hearts. After all, anything could happen. Birthmothers have been known to change their minds even up to and including in the delivery room, and we didn't want to see Jan's heart broken again.

But over the next several months, Jan and Steve formed a deep bond with the woman who wrote that e-mail message, and with her brave daughter. On February 16, 1998, they all gathered at a hospital in Memphis to witness the birth of Jan and Steve's son, Matthew Aaron Easley.

Matthew couldn't come to Jan and Steve the traditional way, so he had to work a little harder to find a way to get to them. He deserves a rest. Perhaps a nice nap in the sun on the boat, with the gentle rocking of the waves, will do the trick. In fact, I think I'll join him.

Flora Abunda...

It is June, and the clover is in bloom.

In the Midwest, clover grows in abundance nearly everywhere you look, and is considered by many little more than cattle feed. I, too, had taken it for granted for most of my life. It's one of those things you don't even notice, like the Queen Anne's Lace that grows in ditches by the side of the road, its delicate blossoms bravely surviving despite subsisting on a diet of litter and exhaust fumes. But we aren't trained to notice things like wildflowers. We tend to judge things by their material worth, not their intrinsic beauty. In my youth, I fully bought in to this capitalistic view of the natural world, believing that even pretty flowers weren't worth much unless you could do something with them, like put them under your chin to see if you liked butter.

Then I moved out West for a few years. I've talked about our move earlier, and so it's no secret how deeply it affected me to be for a few years in a climate and landscape that was so fundamentally different than the one I've known most of my life. Before we moved, I was unaware that even some plants and animals that had the same names as their counterparts in the Midwest would be subtly different. The squirrels that begged at our door in Palo Alto were scrawny and black, not like the glossy fat gray things that sneak into our bird feeders at home. The things called "blue jays" had black pointed crests on their heads. In fact, most of the plants and trees were so unfamiliar to me that it gave me a kind of vertigo. When I went out early to interview for jobs, I spent the night after a great interview which later resulted in a great job in the bathroom, alternately being sick and sobbing with fear. What was I getting myself into, moving to a place where I couldn't even recognize the trees?

It didn't take me long before I grew to appreciate my new surroundings. I marveled at the fact that we could sit outside every night until long after sunset and not awake in the morning covered with mosquito bites. Our first December in California, we opened our Christmas stockings sitting on beach towels in shorts and t-shirts, and sent pictures back of that grand event to our envious friends shivering in below zero temperatures. Our trip even made me more observant and tolerant of other alien life forms we would encounter in future travels, like the yucca in the Arizona desert, kudzu in Georgia or the little blackbird with an orange beak in Italy that had a wider repertoire than our mockingbirds. I grew so spoiled and bold that I grandly announced to Michael that I would move back to the Midwest, but only under the conditions of central air conditioning and an attached garage, so we could at least temper our return to the more adverse weather conditions with some creature comforts that would isolate us from them.

Ellen Rosewall

But when we crossed over the Rockies and entered the Great Plains in June of 1992, I realized I was close to being home again, and as we passed by acres of rich brown earth newly planted with corn and beans, I had to suppress an urge to stop the car, run into a field and bury my hands in Midwestern soil. I contented myself with admiring the profuse displays of purple flowers that covered hillsides by the side of the road at exit ramps and between the farms. What were those incredibly beautiful flowers, and what visionary Nebraska official had started the beautification program that resulted in their being planted everywhere I looked?

The next time we stopped for gas, I saw some up close and realized that the showpiece flowers were just lowly clover. I laughed a bit at the fact that all it took was a 2,000 mile trip to make me appreciate them. And now, every June, I smile with deep satisfaction as I pass the clover by the side of the road in the Midwest. I stop and stare at the Queen Anne's lace, black-eyed Susan and chicory as I walk down the back road behind the cottage. And I assure each flower I meet that I will never take it for granted again.

DEAR LAKE

•••

Dear Lake,

Last weekend I went to a conference that was held at a Dominican retreat center in Southwestern Wisconsin. I was relishing the trip – I was going to be studying something I loved with interesting people surrounded by nature, art and silence. What could be better?

But on the morning after the first day I awoke with a vague sense of unease. There were of course no televisions or radios in our small, dorm-style rooms, and I woke up and got dressed in complete silence. In my household, with three busy, outgoing and musical people, there is seldom silence, and I wouldn't have it any other way. I have grown used to bracketing my sleep with news programs. Even when I travel, a familiar cable channel or a morning news show maintains a sense of familiar noise. Here, I was completely alone. And I didn't like it very much.

Since I have an active (some would say overstimulated) brain I started to think about what this all meant. I noticed that my brain, bereft of music for over 24 hours, created its own by playing Chopin's *Waltz in A Minor*. I started involuntarily seeking mental stimulation by cataloging items in the room ("look, a door stop! I didn't notice that before."). Nothing worked... until I opened the blinds and looked out on a beautiful scene – the complete nothingness of dense fog. Suddenly, the fear and unease disappeared. In an ironic reversal, the fog for me had the same effect that a foghorn would have were I lost in it. Suddenly I was standing at the big picture window at the cottage the morning after a rain storm, gazing out over what the day before were rolling hills covered with cows, pigs and corn and feeling as though the nothingness in front of me could just as easily hide a boathouse, lake and the cottages on the opposite shore.

Although my "winter world" doesn't allow me to stop time very often, at the cottage I can stand motionless in front of a blanket of fog for the longest time and not even notice how long I've been there. So it was in Southwestern Wisconsin, and with the fog as my anchor I could turn back into the room and get back to contemplating the start of the day.

They say that silence is good for you, but as soon as I felt as though I were on familiar ground I started to hear things. It wasn't quiet at all – there was the chirping of sparrows and the cry of killdeer. There was the drip of moisture from the roof, and the sound of a breeze moving through the trees. Down the hall, a hair dryer was blowing, and gradually the faint sounds of my fellow conferees walking down the hall to the bathroom became more noticeable. I sighed with relief...another noise to add to the day.

Ellen Rosewall

I will spend the days until I see you again dreaming of fog...

Love,

me

Handyman's Special...

One of the reasons that the cottage has held up so well for a hundred years is because it has had the loving input of dozens of hands: repairing, updating and improving nearly every corner of the house and property. Sometimes we get professionals to do the work, like when the new roof needed to be put on or the back yard needed to be terraced and drains put in to prevent the soil from eroding down into our back door. But more often, we've done the work ourselves, and now it is impossible to be anywhere at Ja-Ma-Ca without remembering friends and relatives who have contributed to what it is today.

You'd have to pay a pretty penny today to get something as magnificent as our big pine dining room table, but we didn't – it was made by Aunt Jane's father-in-law before I was born. Next to it sits a corner cabinet that was built by my father and Edward Whipps. It originally served as a liquor cabinet in the days when every well-stocked house had to have one, but now it holds our tools and bird feeder supplies.

Aunt Carolyn and Uncle Dick put in the flagstones by the side of the house, and Michael put in the ones that lead from the front porch to the boathouse. Most of us have put in at least some time painting the railings on the porch and boathouse roof. One summer, we hauled some old metal porch chairs out from underneath the porch, and Linda and Michael drilled a couple of drainage holes in the seats so they wouldn't rust any further, sanded and repaired the rust, and painted them a lovely forest green. The next time they needed a touch up, Peter did the repainting. That may have been the same summer that Charlie replaced a couple of rotting spots on the front porch with new tongue-and-groove, Linda painted it and I learned what tongue-and-groove meant.

Linda, who for some reason seems to gain energy on vacation, also made some new living and dining room curtains with some help from Mom and a visiting friend, Joy Jenkins. We were all very grateful, for even though the new curtains were made from bedsheets (shhh - don't tell anyone!), they replaced chintz curtains that had gone out of style in oh, say 1930 or so.

Charlie usually does a good deal of puttering around every summer. Most years, the septic tank needs a little bit of work so Charlie digs out around it and checks it over a bit before the repairman, who we call Joe Septic, arrives. The year of the roof, he got up there and walked around for awhile, but Mom has forbidden future forays up there, so he has to content himself with septic evaluation and the occasional weed-whacking.

Before the new roof was finished, we accumulated several water spots upstairs, and our wonderful friends and frequent visitors the Kies spent a good part of their vacation one year painting the walls

Ellen Rosewall

and sloped ceilings to cover them. The Kies have also contributed some treasured home decor, including a little chalkboard that Linda made which hangs by the back door. Intended for messages, Lynda Kies wrote "Welcome to Heaven!" on it about ten years ago and we haven't had the heart to erase it.

Steve has contributed his expertise to installing a set of garden lights down the back steps that come on automatically at twilight, and creating the Front Porch Branch of Ellen and Jan's offices with an out-door electrical outlet.

Oh, and when you visit, be sure and notice our eclectic collection of original artwork, which includes two handpainted maps of the vicinity (one by Uncle Dick and one by neighbor Downey Moore), some counted cross stitch (a gift in thanks for the Just The Girls week-end), a dream catcher made by Mom and a large macrame owl by Jan.

Me? Well, a disastrous attempt at sewing a pair of shorts with Grandmother's sewing machine when I was in eighth grade con-vinced me that my most effective role in the home improvement process is supervisory. So, over the years, I've taken careful notes. And now I'm writing about it.

Untold Riches...

One Sunday in Bay View, the preacher told this story:

There was once a successful businessman who went on vacation to Mexico. There he ran into a simple fisherman. Not being able to imagine a life so different, he asked the fisherman what he did to pass his days. "Every morning, I go out and catch enough fish to meet my family's needs for the day," said the fisherman. "Then I go back home, cook and eat the fish, have a siesta with my wife, sit on the beach for awhile, and play my guitar."

Well, the businessman was incredulous, but also excited by the untapped potential evident in the fisherman's life. He asked the fisherman why he didn't catch more fish than he needed each day. "What good would that do?" said the fisherman. "You can sell those fish to others, and make enough money to move to Mexico City," said the businessman. "Then you can expand your fishing business and open subsidiaries." "What good would that do?" the fisherman asked again. "You could expand until you had to move to San Diego," said the businessman, warming to his plan. "From there, you would grow and grow, and make more and more money, and then eventually you could move to New York, run your entire operation from there, and sell fish all over the world."

"What good would that do?" the fisherman asked once more. "Well, then you could retire," said the businessman, a bit annoyed that the fisherman wasn't able to grasp even the most simple goal of American capitalism.

"What would I do then?" the fisherman asked.

"Well, you could go live on the beach, catch a few fish, have siestas with your wife and play your guitar any time you wanted to," said the businessman.

Cottages on Walloon Lake don't come up for sale very often, but occasionally there is a cottage owner who moves their winter home too far away to get back easily or dies without heirs, and in those cases the cottages usually sell quickly and for top dollar. Sometimes, people buy cottages of the vintage of Ja-Ma-Ca for astronomical sums, then rip them out and build more modern homes. When this happens, we are always astonished – not only at the mentality that those cottages are so worthless they could be disposed of like used tissues, but also at the fact that there are people in this world that have so much money that they can afford to purchase expensive property and spend hundreds of thousands more to change it until it suits them.

We have no intention of selling our cottage, but every time we hear of a property on Walloon being sold, we roll the purchase price around in our brains for just a little while and imagine what those riches would be able to bring to our lives.

We allow as how it would enable us to purchase some lakefront property, sit on the dock, catch a few fish, and take siestas any time we wanted to.

An Amen Moment...

It was a bright, beautiful, Sparkle Island kind of day.

Jan and Steve had been preparing for days, writing out recipes and duties, making salads, and cleaning the cottage. As the time approached, we set the table, put baby Matthew in his new outfit and greeted the guests. In addition to all of us, we had quite a few family members who were at Walloon Lake for one reason or another and were able to join us. Bunny and Chuck Hyatt, related to Mom through Grandfather's second marriage, bought a home at Walloon after spending several vacations at Ja-Ma-Ca when Grandfather married Chuck's mother. They were joined by their daughter Lynne Kishler and her family. D.A. Kreinbihl, Mom's cousin who had summered next door in her childhood and still takes every opportunity to return, came with her daughters Anne Huber and Beth Kerlin and Beth's children. Rev. Bob and Bettirae Kimes were our special guests by lucky circumstance. Rev. Kimes had been our family's minister in Columbus during the 70s, and even though we've been through a lot of ministers all over the country since then, we've always considered Bob "our" minister. Since he had just taken a summer job at Bay View, it seemed perfect that he would be able to perform the ceremony.

Twenty-two human friends and family were present, but we were attended also by our non-human friends and dear ones: the birds that frequented our feeders, the rocks that lined the path and the trees that bent gracefully over the cottage. The lake shimmered, the birds sang merrily and I would not have been surprised to have turned around and seen a few chipmunks lined up at attention watching the procedure.

When we were all gathered, Peter ran down to the lake and collected water in a little pottery bowl supplied by Rev. Kimes. Jan, Steve, Rev. Kimes and Matthew stood on the front porch steps while we arranged ourselves at the bottom of the steps looking up at them. Emily Kishler was given the pottery baptismal font, and held it high and steady, her face glowing with responsibility. Steve held Matthew in his arms, Jan pressed her lips together to try to stave off the tears so she wouldn't miss anything, and we began.

As the universe stopped to observe, Rev. Kimes dipped his fingers in the Walloon water and traced Matthew's forehead with the ancient symbol of protection and belonging. Then, he explained an African tradition of validating a child's life by proclaiming the name out loud three times for all to hear. "Matthew!" he cried, and his baritone resonated through the trees. "Matthew!" he cried, and the sound carried down to the water. "Matthew!" he cried again, and our hearts resounded with the presence of the new soul among us.

All of this happened, as D.A. would later say, "with nuthin' between us and God." An "amen moment," said Rev. Kimes. And we all knew that Matthew's baptism was more than just his formal welcome into our tribe. It was a confirmation of our oneness with all our relations, the two legged, four legged, winged, flowing, and planted ones who shared space at this most special of places.

It was one of the most sacred moments of our lives.

I'll Gladly Pay You Tuesday for a Memory Today...

I t's fun dredging up old memories at any time. But when the memory-fest is taking place with cousins you haven't seen in years, and the memories involve childhood times at the cottage, family and food – well, that just adds a special spice to the mix.

The "family" in question were our cousins on Mom's side, daughter, grandchildren and great-grandchildren of Mom's Aunt Do and Uncle Alan, who for many years owned the cottage next door. We had taken care of Matthew's baptism earlier in the day, and were settling in with "just one more" glass of wine as the sun set across the lake. While the little ones played on the porch, we remembered our own childhoods: the time Linda and Bethie pretended they were horses and the adults kept getting in trouble by calling them by their human names, the time

SPARKLE ISLAND

Mom and D.A. staged a wedding in the woods and D.A. stormed off because they "weren't doing it right," the time we put on a show and Uncle Alan gave us each a fifty-cent piece. The memories were flying fast and furious, until one memory stopped us cold.

Wimpy's, said one of us, with a reverent hush. Remember Wimpy's?

Now, granted, we are a family who loves our food, but there is still something unnatural about an entire roomful of people falling into drooling blobs at the mere mention of a tiny hamburger joint that has been closed for more than thirty years.

We could not remember the names Linda and Bethie called themselves when they were horses, but we could see clearly the waxy white butcher paper that wrapped the hamburgers, with ends folded neatly underneath. We could not piece together any of the musical numbers that were performed in our show, but we could rattle off Wimpy's menu in unison: The Standard (a hamburger with mayonnaise and olives, my personal favorite), The Regular (with ketchup, mustard, pickles and chopped onion) and The Deluxe, a Regular with lettuce and tomato. And milkshakes. That's all. No fries, onion rings or other accompaniments, because apparently the hamburger was all you needed. We even remember the hamburgers as costing ten cents, a price that is burned into our collective memories even though it had to be higher than that, at least in the later years.

Wimpy's was a true Mom and Pop operation – Wimpy (at least we called him that, we never knew his real name) cooked while his wife came out to your car, took your order and brought it back to you on a plastic tray that hooked on to the half open window on the driver's side. They never wrote your order down, and they never got anything wrong. They didn't worry about modern notions like plastic smiles and encouraging their customers to "Have a good day," they just served hamburgers – fast, hot and good. When Wimpy died, his wife tried to keep the business going with their son, but it just wasn't the same. By that time, golden arches and other mass-produced hamburger chains had appeared on the scene and it was hard for a small time business to keep up.

A bank now sits on the former Wimpy's site. There is one of those hamburger chain restaurants on the opposite corner. We go there often. We like the food a lot. But I couldn't tell you what the proprietor looks like. And I'm fairly certain I won't reminisce about the experience thirty years from now.

DEAR LAKE

•••

Dear Lake,

This morning, there was a beautiful pink spot right in the middle of you when the rising sun peeked from behind a cloud to leave its reflection. Yesterday, we had a great sparkle island that extended from the opposite shore right to our dock. The day before, it was rainy, and your surface was gray and pockmarked by raindrops.

Over the years, I imagine that I've seen just about all of the moods it is possible for you to have. I've come down in the early morning and seen you calm and clear as glass. I've seen you covered with fog, churned up like an angry whitecapped river or undulating gently in invitation. You've been deep blue, green, gray and even purple. Sometimes, you are striated with the waves of passing power boats or wind lines. Most days, we can clearly see the dropoff where our sandbar ends and you get deep, but some days the line is obscured by choppy waves or dreary gray weather.

I think I know you. But, of course, I'm only seeing your surface. Which is the real you, the part that I can see or what lies underneath? Am I treating you like humans sometimes treat each other, looking at the outside and not even bothering to probe the depths for the complexities within?

Sometimes I get frustrated at other humans, including and even especially the ones who have known me for a long time. Don't they know me by now? I say. Why don't they understand me? But other times I realize that there are parts of me that even I don't fully understand. What makes me able to run a successful business and not be able to push a plate away when there's still food on it? Why do I snap and bark at someone one day and have infinite patience the next?

I've found, throughout my life, that when I wonder these things, it helps to sit on the front porch or on the dock and just look at you for a long time, listening and waiting. It is those times when I come to know that it doesn't matter what is beneath the surface, it just matters that we respect that there is something. And at least by listening and waiting, that we can come closer to understanding than by talking all the time.

Love,

me

The Journey North ~ Part II...

In September 5, 1998, in the 46th year of my life, at about 6:00 in the evening Eastern Standard Time, I saw something I had never ever seen before: leaves beginning to turn color over Walloon Lake.

When I was growing up, coming back to the cottage in the fall was just not an option. Our two weeks were allotted by Grandfather and Grandmother's schedule, and with only that big oil heater the cottage wasn't well equipped to handle us much beyond August. And besides, once September rolled around, school was back in session and our thoughts, and schedules, had turned to other things.

Once Mom put in the LP gas furnace, she began to stay past Labor Day, and usually tried to get back at least once in October as well. She began sharing stories of pleasures I could only imagine: building a fire in the fireplace nearly every night, walking down the back road as leaves gently fell on the path, bundling up in fall sweaters and coats, visiting our favorite sites unencumbered by the tourist crowds of summer. But by that time, I was living in Minneapolis, and in those days of graduate school and beginning my life with Michael, time and budget made more than one trip per year impossible. While Michael was in graduate school in California, our meager teacher's budget turned into a slim-to-none student's budget, and we didn't even make it back to the Midwest for the duration of our time there.

So when we announced in the early 90s that we were moving to Green Bay, the first thing Mom said was that we now would be able to come to the cottage any time we wanted. We imagined shuttling across the Upper Peninsula several times during the summer; opening the cottage as soon as the ice was off the lake and lingering far into the fall. But even with the cottage only five and a half hours away it seemed as though one trip per year was all that we managed to fit in.

In August of this year, however, I had just completed a major project and was weary, physically and mentally. I badly needed a few days off, and when I learned that Mom, Charlie and Linda were all gathering at the cottage for Labor Day weekend, my throat began to hurt with the longing to be there too. Bless my dear husband, who has never been the kind of man to assume that we all go or no one goes – and since he was getting ready for the start of school, I packed my single bag, loaded my jackets and sweaters into the car and headed north for the second time that season.

Sure, it was only Labor Day weekend, hardly even fall in most of the country, but already the signs of change were evident in the northwoods. As I drove across Highway 2, several maples were already tinged with yellow, and the gentle wind had already coaxed more than a few leaves from their comfortable summer homes. The sun, weary from the hard work of the summer, had relaxed a little in the sky and the water had cooled to a deep cobalt. As I pulled up to the cottage, everything seemed different. The back porch light shed a more golden glow on the back steps, and the light from within radiated coziness and warmth.

My normal ritual upon arriving at the cottage is to run down the steps to the lake and trail my fingers in the water in delicious anticipation of refreshing afternoon dips. This time, I found myself stopping at the front porch, gazing out over the water. The sunset had started, and even the oranges and pinks that filled the sky seemed warmer, rounder, more friendly, than their July counterparts.

I slowly lowered myself into the Hemingway chair and instead of dipping my fingers in lake water I brushed tears off my cheeks.

Life is good when you have a wonderful husband, a good marriage, a son who makes you proud, a business that is going well enough to leave you exhausted every once in awhile, and time now and again to take a long weekend.

Life is good when you have a lake to look at, a front porch to sit on and a loving family inside the cottage.

Life is good when you can come home any time you want to.

And every night, when parents started calling from various cottages, Jane, Mary and Carolyn and all of their neighbors would sing:

Day is done
Gone the sun
From the lakes,
    From the hills,
        From the sky,
All is well,
Safely rest,
God is nigh.

Now run along home
And jump into bed
Say your prayers and cover your head.
This very same thing
I say unto you
You dream of me
And I'll dream of you.

ELLEN ROSEWALL has been going to Ja-Ma-Ca on Walloon Lake since she was six months old. Since then, she has commuted to the cottage from homes in Columbus Ohio; Minneapolis, Minnesota; Palo Alto, California; and De Pere, Wisconsin. She lives in De Pere with her husband, Michael, and son, Peter. She spends her winter months consulting for arts and cultural organizations and dreaming of Walloon.